S0-CAW-794

CAFÉ & BAKERY

# LA BOULANGE

# CAFÉ
# COOKING

## AT HOME

Enjoy!

Pascal.

CAFÉ & BAKERY

# LA BOULANGE

# CAFÉ
# COOKING

## AT HOME

FOREWORD BY
HOWARD SCHULTZ

. . . . . . . . . . . . . . . . . . . .

BY
PASCAL RIGO
*and the*
CHEFS AND BAKERS *of*
LA BOULANGE

. . . . . . . . . . . . . . . .

PHOTOGRAPHS BY
DAVID VERGNE

| CHEF DE CUISINE | PASTRY CHEF | BOOK PRODUCER | DESIGNER |
| ALAIN BOURGADE | STEPHANE STOCKI | LEAH DONNELLY | ALYSSA WARNOCK |

This edition published exclusively for Bay Bread LLC
by Chronicle Books LLC.

Copyright © 2012 by Bay Bread LLC.

All rights reserved. No part of this book may be reproduced
in any form without written permission from the publisher.

ISBN: 978-1-4521-2000-3

Manufactured in China.

Production design by Cat Grishaver.

Tabasco is a registered trademark of McIlhenny Company.

10 9 8 7 6 5 4 3 2 1

Chronicle Books LLC
680 Second Street
San Francisco, California 94107

www.chroniclebooks.com/custom

# CONTENTS

✧

# FOREWORD

The best relationships often feel like they were destined to happen, a fated meeting of personalities, values, and aspirations. Such connections taste oddly familiar, as if a partnership was meant to be.

I was a fan of La Boulange Café and Bakery long before I first met its dynamic founder, Pascal Rigo, and the two of us sat down at his dining room table for a home-cooked meal of baked halibut, lentil stew, and, of course, freshly baked bread. Over dinner, as we shared our respective histories, I came to fully understand why La Boulange cafés had so deeply resonated with me. Just as Starbucks has always been about so much more than coffee, La Boulange stands for much more than fine baked goods. In this and other respects, Pascal and I are truly kindred spirits.

Despite being born an ocean apart, we were each raised in similarly modest circumstances—Pascal in the port city of Bordeaux, France, and I in the projects of Brooklyn, New York. When the time came to pursue our respective dreams, each of us looked to America's West Coast. To Los Angeles and San Francisco, Pascal brought his love and knowledge of French baking, initially selling baguettes under a hand-painted awning, a small endeavor that grew into multiple beloved cafés. To Seattle, I brought my love and deep appreciation for the romance of Italian espresso bars, which I discovered during one of my first business trips abroad, and tried to re-create along the streets of the Pacific Northwest. Our businesses grew, I believe, because of the genuine love that each of us had, and still has, for our companies, as well as our expectations of and respect for the people with whom we work.

That love and respect were evident when I toured La Boulange's stores and central bakery with Pascal. Watching him taste croissants and speak with his colleagues was to watch a maestro at work! I was struck immediately by his high standards and the pride he took in creating an uncompromising customer experience. It became clear that Pascal's commitment to the quality of La Boulange's French-inspired artisanal fare would complement Starbucks's own commitment to sourcing and roasting the highest-quality coffee, and crafting the perfect beverage. Our shared values and our businesses' cultural similarities seemed to imply a fated fit. Pascal and I decided to unite our two companies and create what we believe is a uniquely special food and beverage pairing.

It is never easy to bring a culinary product from one part of the world to another, let alone interpret a premium culinary experience on a grand scale. Yet as anyone who has walked through its doors and sat at its tables can attest, La Boulange already has succeeded in capturing the essence of France's signature cafés. And although the European origins of my and Pascal's entrepreneurial visions differ, the French café and the Italian espresso bar do share a universally important quality: the potential to bring people together.

Inspiring human connections—whether it's over the perfect croissant, or the perfect cup of coffee, or both—is the true power of any food or beverage. On this Pascal and I humbly agree, and it is my hope that the recipes he shares on the following pages will have a similar effect in your own home—bringing your family, friends, and neighbors together over a fantastic meal.

HOWARD SCHULTZ
chairman, president, and ceo
Starbucks Coffee Company

# INTRODUCTION

This book has been several years in the making. Soon after we published our first book, *The American Boulangerie* (2003), I was excited about working on a book of recipes that explored our café menu beyond breads, pastries, and desserts. I have always loved the idea of a photocentric cookbook, but it wasn't until we started putting together step-by-step photo instructions for making our monthly specials, which we use to train our cooks, that the concept for this book really came alive.

Each of the recipes in *Café Cooking at Home* is illustrated by a series of photos that guides the reader through the cooking process. For many home cooks, it is helpful to *see* what a properly seared cube of beef looks like or what the consistency of a reduction should be, rather than just reading about it. The book covers everything from simple salads like our classic Caesar (page 61) to our La Boulange monthly specials such as Chicken Tagine (page 153) to the desserts that we serve at our La Boulange Fridays fund-raisers, like Cannelés with Caramelized Bananas (page 167). They range from very simple basics, like Caramelized Onions (page 195), to more complex preparations of meats and fish. My hope is that the beautiful photos will become helpful kitchen tools as you make your way through the cookbook.

One of the best things about preparing a dish at home is being able to adapt it. If you prefer turkey bacon to pork, or you have romaine lettuce on hand instead of frisée, go ahead and use what you like or what you have in your refrigerator or pantry. We want these recipes to fit into your busy life and become staples in your home. We hope to bring the new, the old, and the classic from La Boulange Café and Bakery into your home, so that you can share this wonderful food with friends and family.

# BREAKFAST & BRUNCH

# CRUNCHY GRANOLA

## GRANOLA

*Makes 4 to 6 cups*

This is one of our signature items at La Boulange. We've been making it since the beginning. We thought long and hard about giving up this recipe, but we know that you really want it, so here it is. What makes this granola so delicious is the maple syrup. And its crunchiness is also key, so make sure you bake it thoroughly. It's great with yogurt, fruit and honey, on ice cream, or all by itself.

### ‹ INGREDIENTS ›

- ½ cup coarsely chopped walnuts
- ⅓ cup dry-roasted almonds
- ¼ cup shelled sunflower seeds
- 3 cups rolled (old-fashioned) oats
- ¼ cup all-purpose flour
- ¼ teaspoon salt
- ½ cup canola oil
- ½ cup maple syrup

1. Gather your ingredients. Preheat the oven to 350°F.

2. In a large bowl, mix all the dry ingredients together. Add the canola oil and maple syrup and toss so everything is well coated.

3. Spray a large baking sheet with nonstick canola oil spray. Spread out the mixture evenly. Bake for 30 to 35 minutes, stirring every 10 minutes.

### ‹ KITCHEN NOTES ›

- The granola can be eaten right away or stored for several weeks in an airtight container or jar.
- Add dried fruit, chocolate chips, coconut shavings—whatever you like!
- If you like your granola with large clusters, stir lightly.

# FANTASTIC FRENCH TOAST

## PAIN PERDU

*Makes 12 muffin-size French toasts*

This is one of the top sellers at La Boulange. These muffin-size French toasts take a little longer to make than traditional French toast, but they're well worth it. Serve with a few slices of Canadian bacon or English breakfast sausages—what a fantastic breakfast!

### ◄ INGREDIENTS ►

- Butter for greasing the muffin pan
- 8 slices (1-inch thick) Brioche or plain white sandwich bread
- 1 cup whole milk
- 1 cup heavy cream
- ½ cup sugar
- 3 eggs
- ¼ teaspoon vanilla extract
- Confectioners' sugar for dusting
- Warm maple syrup for serving
- Mixed fresh berries for serving

1. Gather your ingredients. Preheat the oven to 350°F. Butter a 12-cup muffin pan.

2. Cut the brioche into a large dice. You should have 5 to 6 cups of diced bread.

3. In a large bowl, whisk together the milk, cream, and sugar, and then whisk in the eggs and vanilla.

4. Add the bread cubes, stir well, and allow the bread to soak for 10 minutes.

5. Spoon the mixture into the muffin pan, dividing it evenly among the cups. Bake for 35 minutes or until golden brown.

6. Remove from the pan, dust with confectioners' sugar, and serve warm with maple syrup and mixed berries.

### ◄ KITCHEN NOTES ►

- Use focaccia bread instead of brioche.
- Add a few blueberries and a little bit of grated lemon zest along with the bread cubes before baking.
- Drizzle with honey instead of serving with maple syrup.
- Serve with ice cream for a great dessert.
- The French toast can be made in advance, cooled, wrapped well, and frozen for several weeks. Reheat in a microwave for 2 minutes or in a 350°F oven for 10 minutes or until heated through.

# OMELETTE DE PARIS

*Serves 1*

This is a super-traditional French dish, typically served as a light lunch or dinner. The omelet is best when the eggs are beaten really well, so that they are very light and airy. Delicious with a green salad with a mustard vinaigrette.

## ◄ INGREDIENTS ►

- 4 button mushrooms
- 2 slices Serrano ham
- 1 tablespoon canola oil
- ½ cup baby spinach
- 2 eggs
- Salt and freshly ground pepper

1. Gather your ingredients.

2. Clean and slice the mushrooms. Coarsely chop the ham.

3. In a nonstick medium skillet over medium heat, heat the canola oil and sauté the spinach until slightly wilted.

4. Add the ham and mushrooms and continue to sauté for another minute.

5. In a bowl, whisk the eggs well and season with salt and pepper. Pour the eggs into your hot pan.

6. Let the eggs set for 1 to 2 minutes. Once they begin to turn golden on the bottom, fold omelet in half and serve.

## ◄ KITCHEN NOTES ►

- Substitute chopped avocado or any veggies you have on hand in your fridge. Add grated Swiss cheese at the end.
- Brush top with a little Gorgonzola cheese.
- Sprinkle with toasted pine nuts.

# LA BOULANGE SALAD

## LA SALADE DE LA BOULANGE

*Serves 1*

This La Boulange twist on the famous salade Lyonnaise features fried eggs instead of the traditional poached. It's a complete lunch or dinner on its own, and, though it may sound strange, it makes a great breakfast. For the best eating experience, break the fried eggs and mix the runny yolks into the salad so that they coat the greens, bacon, and croutons.

### ◄ INGREDIENTS ►

- 1 teaspoon unsalted butter
- 2 slices bacon, cut crosswise into pieces
- 2 eggs
- Salt and freshly ground pepper
- 1 small head frisée
- ⅓ cup Croutons (page 196) made with brioche
- Balsamic Vinaigrette (page 199)

1. Gather your ingredients.

2. Melt the butter in a medium skillet over medium heat and add the bacon. Cook, stirring occasionally, until browned and lightly crisped. Transfer to a plate. Pour off most of the fat and return the skillet to medium heat.

3. Break the eggs into the skillet and season with salt and pepper. Cook until the whites are set and slightly golden on the edges. Don't overcook your yolks, which are the best part.

4. Transfer the eggs to a plate.

5. Arrange the frisée on the plate, around the eggs.

6. Scatter the bacon and croutons on top, drizzle with vinaigrette, and serve right away.

### ◄ KITCHEN NOTES ►

- Frisée is the best green to use for this salad, but other types will work, too.
- Replace the bacon with turkey bacon or with chicken seared in butter.
- Warm the vinaigrette before tossing.

# CROQUE MONSIEUR *or* MADAME

*Serves 2*

This is a decadent version of a classic French sandwich because we use béchamel instead of butter or crème fraîche. The quality of the ham is important, and nice thin slices are best. Wonderful on Sunday night, watching a game or winding down after the weekend.

## ⊰ INGREDIENTS ⊱

- ¼ cup plus 2 tablespoons Béchamel Sauce (page 203)
- 4 slices *pain de mie*, country bread, or brioche, toasted
- 4 slices Serrano ham
- ½ cup shredded Gruyère cheese
- 1 egg (for a Madame)

1. Gather your ingredients. Preheat the broiler to 450°F.

2. Spread 1 tablespoon of béchamel on one side of each slice of toasted bread. Layer 2 slices of bread with the ham and cover with the remaining bread.

3. Spread the remaining béchamel on the tops of the sandwiches and sprinkle with the Gruyère cheese. Broil for 1 to 2 minutes to finish. For a Madame, fry an egg and lay it on top.

## ⊰ KITCHEN NOTES ⊱
- The Monsieur can be prepared in advance, wrapped well, and frozen.

# EGG & CHEESE SANDWICH

## CROISSANTS AUX OEUFS, BACON ET FROMAGE

*Serves 2*

These are comforting, super-simple, *super bon* sandwiches, perfect for breakfast, brunch, lunch, and even dinner.
Serve them with fresh fruit, Boulange Potatoes (page 129), or a simple green salad.

### ⌐ INGREDIENTS ⌐

- 2 flaky, all-butter croissants
- 2 slices thick-cut bacon
- 2 eggs
- Salt and freshly ground pepper
- ½ cup shredded Swiss cheese (or any cheese you like)

1. Gather your ingredients.

2. Cut each croissant in half horizontally.

3. In a small skillet over medium-high heat, fry the bacon until crisp on both sides. Transfer to a plate and set aside, leaving the fat in the pan.

4. Break the eggs into the skillet over medium heat and scramble with a wooden spoon. Cook to your desired consistency. Season with salt and pepper to taste.

5. Divide the eggs between the two bottom halves of the croissants. Lay a slice of bacon on top of the eggs.

6. Sprinkle with cheese, cover with the croissant tops, and serve.

### ⌐ KITCHEN NOTES ⌐

- Use slices of brioche instead of croissants.
- Add a slice of avocado or ripe tomato to each sandwich.
- Substitute smoked salmon or grilled vegetables for the bacon.
- Replace the Swiss with Morbier cheese.

# EGG SALAD SANDWICH
## SANDWICH AUX OEUFS

*Serves 2*

An egg salad with tarragon, cornichons, and capers—how can we go wrong?

### ⤙ INGREDIENTS ⤚

- 3 hard-boiled eggs
- 8 cornichons
- 2 tablespoons capers
- 2 tablespoons fresh tarragon leaves
- ¼ cup Aioli (page 201)
- Salt and freshly ground pepper
- 4 slices *pain de mie* or white sandwich bread, toasted
- 1 tomato, sliced

1. Gather your ingredients.

2. Remove the egg yolks and crush using the side of your knife. Transfer to a large bowl.

3. Chop the egg whites and add to the bowl.

4. Finely chop the cornichons and add them to the bowl, too.

5. Chop the tarragon and sprinkle over the cornichons. Add the capers, the aioli, salt, and pepper to taste and mix well.

6. Spread the egg salad onto 2 slices of bread. Add the tomato and cover with the remaining bread.

### ⤙ KITCHEN NOTES ⤚

- Use your favorite sandwich bread.
- The egg salad can be eaten on a bed of greens rather than on bread.
- There are 4 eggs in the photo, but we use just 3!
- Make this with just egg whites for a healthy option.

# SMOKED SALMON TARTINE

## TARTINE DE SAUMON FUMÉ

*Serves 1*

A tartine is an open-faced sandwich—just a slice of great bread with tasty toppings. This version, with smoked salmon,
is simple but elegant, and ideal for brunch or a light lunch. Quality is important, but remember that sometimes the best ingredients
are what you can find or what you can afford, so keep it simple and keep it fresh.

### ◄ INGREDIENTS ►

- 1 small shallot
- 1 cucumber
- 2 tablespoons crème fraîche

- Juice of ½ lemon
- Salt and freshly ground pepper

- 1 slice country bread
- 2 or 3 slices smoked salmon

- 2 tablespoons capers
- Fresh dill sprigs

1. Gather your ingredients.

2. Peel and finely chop the shallot and set aside.

3. Cut a few thin slices from the cucumber.

4. Mix the crème fraîche with the lemon juice, salt, and pepper.

5. Spread the crème fraîche on the bread and lay the slices of cucumber and smoked salmon on top.

6. Sprinkle with the shallot and capers and garnish with fresh dill sprigs. Serve right away.

### ◄ KITCHEN NOTES ►

- Use thinly sliced red onions instead of the shallot.
- Add a dash or two of your favorite hot sauce to spice things up.
- Replace the capers with finely chopped cornichons.
- Use regular or low-fat cream cheese in place of crème fraîche.

# HUMMUS & AVOCADO TARTINE

### TARTINE HUMMUS ET AVOCAT

*Serves 1*

This tartine is healthy, light, and bright. Wonderful with a cup of soup.

### ◄ INGREDIENTS ►

- 2 tablespoons hummus
- 1 slice country bread
- 5 slices cucumber

- 1 tomato, sliced
- ½ avocado, sliced

- 2 to 3 tablespoons sprouts
- Salt and freshly ground pepper

- 1 tablespoon extra-virgin olive oil

1. Gather your ingredients.

2. Spread the hummus on the bread and lay the cucumber and tomato slices on top.

3. Cover with the avocado. Sprinkle with the sprouts, and add salt and pepper to taste. Drizzle with olive oil.

### ◄ KITCHEN NOTES ►

- Sprinkle the Middle Eastern spice blend za'atar or dried or fresh oregano on top.

# SOUPS

# FRENCH ONION SOUP

## SOUPE À L'OIGNON

*Serves* 4

This is a popular soup served in all regions of France and eaten at any time of the day,
from morning to very late at night. It is a very basic soup, and an inexpensive one.

### ⊰ INGREDIENTS ⊱

- 5 onions
- 4 tablespoons unsalted butter
- 1 tablespoon all-purpose flour
- 1 cup white wine
- 4 cups beef broth
- Salt and freshly ground pepper
- 12 slices baguette, toasted
- 2 ounces Gruyère cheese, shredded

1. Gather your ingredients. Preheat the broiler.

2. Thinly slice the onions.

3. Melt the butter in a large pot over medium-high heat and add the onions.

4. Reduce heat to medium-low and cook, stirring occasionally, until the onions are soft and turn a deep brown, 35 to 40 minutes. Add the flour and white wine and stir.

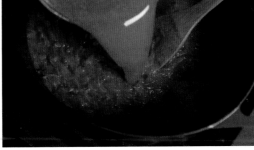

5. Add the beef broth and stir. Add salt and pepper to taste. Cover and cook for 10 minutes.

6. Sprinkle a healthy pinch of grated Gruyère cheese on each toasted baguette slice. Broil for 3 minutes or until the cheese is melted. Top each soup serving with 2 to 3 Gruyère croutons.

### ⊰ KITCHEN NOTES ⊱

- Make the croutons with blue cheese instead of Gruyère. It's crazy good.
- In our book, it's okay to slurp when you eat this soup.

*Soups*

# ROASTED TOMATO SOUP

## SOUPE DE TOMATES

*Serves 2*

This is a particularly flavorful version of tomato soup because of the preparation of the tomatoes. Roasting develops their essence.
It is a summer soup, perfect for a warm evening and delicious served warm or chilled.

### ‹ INGREDIENTS ›

- 6 ripe tomatoes
- 2 garlic cloves, halved
- ¼ cup extra-virgin olive oil, plus more for drizzling
- Salt and freshly ground pepper
- 2 celery ribs, chopped
- 2 tablespoons tomato paste
- 1 cup canned tomato sauce
- ½ vegetable bouillon cube
- 4 fresh basil leaves plus 1 sprig for garnish

1. Gather your ingredients. Preheat the oven to 400°F.

2. Arrange the tomatoes on a baking sheet with the garlic cloves. Drizzle with olive oil and sprinkle each with salt and pepper. Roast for 15 minutes.

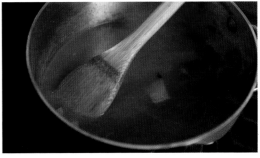

3. While the tomatoes roast, in a pot over medium heat, heat the ¼ cup of olive oil and add the celery and tomato paste. Cook for 2 minutes. Add the tomato sauce and water to cover by ½ inch. Add the bouillon cube. Cook until the celery is tender, about 5 minutes. Transfer to a blender.

4. Add the roasted tomatoes along with the roasting juices and garlic cloves to the blender.

5. Add the basil and puree until smooth. Season with salt and pepper.

6. Pour the soup through a strainer directly into your serving bowl. Drizzle with olive oil and garnish with a basil sprig.

### ‹ KITCHEN NOTES ›

- This soup is tasty with cottage cheese croutons, olive oil, and Pistou (page 204).
- Rub garlic on slices of baguette and broil for a nice garlic crouton.

# PEA SOUP
## SOUPE DE PETITS POIS

*Serves 2*

Of course this soup is delicious during spring, when the peas are in season, but don't be shy to use frozen peas any other time of the year. This soup will surely brighten a cold day and help fight off those cold-weather blues.

### ◄ INGREDIENTS ►

- 1 pound shelled fresh or frozen peas
- 2 tablespoons unsalted butter
- 2 tablespoons extra-virgin olive oil, plus more for drizzling
- Salt and freshly ground pepper
- A few arugula leaves for garnish

1. Gather your ingredients.

2. Cook the peas in a few inches of salted boiling water until they start to rise, 2 to 3 minutes for frozen peas and a little longer for fresh. Drain and put in a blender, making sure to save the cooking water.

3. Add the butter, olive oil, and enough of the cooking water to cover the peas. Blend, adding more of the water to thin to your desired consistency. Add salt and pepper to taste. Drizzle each serving with olive oil and garnish with arugula.

### ◄ KITCHEN NOTES ►
- Add a spoonful of crème fraîche to each serving, and stir very lightly, so that a healthy dollop remains afloat.
- Fantastic with a slice of Potato Tart (page 111).

*Soups*

# WHITE BEAN SOUP

## SOUPE DE HARICOTS BLANCS

*Serves 4*

This is a wonderful fall or winter soup, great with diced sausage or sautéed root vegetables.
And since it is such a hearty soup, it's a delicious meal on its own.

### ⊰ INGREDIENTS ⊱

- 1 onion
- 6 whole cloves
- 1½ pounds dried white beans, soaked overnight in water to cover by 2 inches
- 1 carrot
- 3 bay leaves
- ¼ cup plus 1 tablespoon heavy cream
- 2 tablespoons sherry vinegar
- Vegetable broth to thin the soup (optional)
- Salt and freshly ground pepper
- Cilantro for garnish

1. Gather your ingredients.

2. Peel the onion and stick it with the cloves. In a large pot, combine the beans, carrot, bay leaves, and enough water to cover by 1 inch. Do not add salt at this stage. Bring to a boil, reduce to a simmer, and cook for about 30 minutes, or until the vegetables and beans are soft.

3. Remove the onion, carrot, and bay leaves. With a slotted spoon, transfer the beans to a blender and add cooking liquid to cover. While blending, add the cream, vinegar, and vegetable broth or cooking water to reach your desired consistency. Add salt and pepper to taste. Garnish each serving with cilantro.

### ⊰ KITCHEN NOTES ⊱

- This soup is best made with dried beans that you prepare, but canned beans can be used as well. In that case, you will not need the onion, cloves, carrot, or bay leaves.
- Substitute vegetable broth for the water when cooking the beans.
- Before you puree, you can add a very thick slice of cooked bacon or a piece of cooked ham.
- Cilantro will add a nice kick (sorry, Pierre), but parsley works as well.

# BUTTERNUT SQUASH SOUP
## SOUPE DE COURGE

*Serves 6*

The most amazing thing about this super-simple creamy soup is that there is no cream.
It is made with just three ingredients: butternut squash, butter, and a little extra-virgin olive oil.
This is a good soup to make in large batches and freeze. Enjoy it with a piece of multigrain bread.

### ◄ INGREDIENTS ►

- 4 pounds butternut squash
- ½ cup (1 stick) unsalted butter, cut into pieces
- 2 teaspoons extra-virgin olive oil, or as needed
- Salt and freshly ground pepper

1. Gather your ingredients.

2. Cut each end off the squash and peel. Remove and dispose of the seeds.

3. Cut the squash into 1-inch cubes.

4. Put in a pot of salted boiling water and cook for about 15 minutes or until soft.

5. Transfer the squash to a blender, add the butter, and pour in cooking liquid to cover.

6. Blend, gradually adding more cooking water to reach your desired consistency. Slowly add the olive oil. Add salt and pepper to taste.

### ◄ KITCHEN NOTES ►

- Serve with multigrain croutons or diced sautéed squash.
- Wonderful with sautéed mushrooms.

*Soups*

# FARMER'S SOUP

## POTAGE CULTIVATEUR

❧━◆━❧

*Serves 6 to 8*

This is truly a meal on its own—all you need is a big hunk of country bread to go with it. A comforting soup during winter, it is simple to make and great as a leftover. In an old French farming tradition, when the bowl of soup is nearly finished and just the broth remains, red table wine is added for a few final warming sips before heading back into the fields.

### ◄ INGREDIENTS ►

- 2 leeks, rinsed
- 2 carrots
- 2 waxy potatoes, such as red or Yukon gold
- 1 turnip
- 2 celery ribs
- ¾ cup haricots verts
- ¼ head savoy cabbage
- 3 tablespoons unsalted butter
- 3 slices bacon
- Salt and freshly ground pepper

1. Gather your ingredients.

2. Trim the ends and halve the leeks lengthwise. Thinly slice the white and light green parts and discard the rest.

3. Peel and dice the carrots, potatoes, and turnip. Chop the celery. Cut the haricots verts into ½-inch lengths.

4. Core the cabbage and cut the leaves into thin shreds.

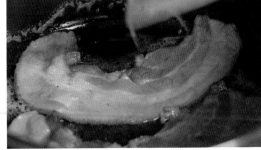

5. Melt the butter in a large pot or Dutch oven over medium heat and add the bacon. Cook until lightly browned, 4 to 5 minutes.

6. Add the leeks and stir to coat with the bacon fat.

7. Add the carrots, potatoes, turnip, celery, and cabbage to the pot.

8. Add just enough water to cover the vegetables and bring to a boil. Cover, reduce the heat to medium-low, and simmer gently. Cook for 1 hour or until the vegetables are tender.

9. Add the haricots verts and cook for 5 minutes or until tender. Season with salt and pepper and serve.

# HERB SOUP
## SOUPE D'HERBES

❖◆❖

*Serves 4*

Full of nutrients, this soup is healthy, cleansing, and simple. All of your guests are sure to enjoy it. This works well warm or cool.

### ◄ INGREDIENTS ►

- ½ onion
- 3 tablespoons unsalted butter

- 3 garlic cloves
- 1 leek
- 1 medium potato
- ½ cup fresh parsley leaves

- ⅓ cup arugula
- ⅓ cup mixed greens
- ⅓ cup frisée
- ½ pound frozen spinach

- 1 to 2 tablespoons extra-virgin olive oil for finishing
- Salt and freshly ground pepper

1. Gather your ingredients.

2. Slice the onion. Melt the butter in a large pot over medium heat and add onion and garlic. Cook for 2 minutes or until the onion is soft and translucent.

3. Meanwhile, rinse the leek and trim the ends. Cut it crosswise into quarters, add to the pot, and cook for 2 minutes.

4. Peel the potato and cut into small cubes. Add to the pot and cook for 8 minutes, stirring occasionally.

5. Add all the greens, and add enough water to cover. Cook for about 15 minutes or until the potatoes are fully cooked.

6. Transfer to a blender in batches and puree. Slowly add olive oil to taste. Season with salt and pepper.

### ◄ KITCHEN NOTES ►

- Use greens that are in season or that you have left over in your refrigerator, such as Swiss chard, to replace the mixed greens.
- Just before serving, drizzle some olive oil to finish.

# CUCUMBER GAZPACHO

## GASPACHO DE CONCOMBRE

*Serves 4 to 6*

Gazpacho is a classic raw summer soup, usually made with tomatoes. We like to use cucumbers to really cool things down. Instead of cream, we use a mix of herbed and regular cream cheeses. Served in small glasses and garnished with diced tomato and shredded mint leaves, this soup is a wonderful appetizer.

### ‹ INGREDIENTS ›

- 1 very large or 2 medium cucumbers
- 3 ounces Boursin cheese with herbs
- 2 ounces cream cheese
- 8 fresh mint leaves
- 1 tablespoon extra-virgin olive oil
- Juice of ½ lemon
- Salt and freshly ground pepper

1. Gather your ingredients.

2. Cut the cucumber in half lengthwise, remove the seeds with a spoon, and cut each half in half again crosswise. Peel 2 or 3 strips off of each cucumber section.

3. Dice the cucumber sections.

4. Transfer the cucumber, cheeses, mint, and olive oil to a blender and blend until smooth. Add lemon juice to taste. Season with salt and pepper and refrigerate until cold.

### ‹ KITCHEN NOTES ›

- Whip some Boursin with a little cream and spoon a dollop into each bowl before serving.
- Great with grilled fish or shrimp.

# SALADS

# CELERY RÉMOULADE

## CÉLERI RÉMOULADE

*Makes 2 to 3 cups*

This is a classic crudité, a raw vegetable dipped or sometimes tossed in a very simple vinaigrette.
At La Boulange, we serve this with our lobster sandwich. It's really the French version of coleslaw.

## ◄ INGREDIENTS ►

- 2 celery roots
- Juice of ½ lemon

- ½ cup Mayonnaise
  (page 201)

1. Gather your ingredients.

2. Cut the ends off each celery root and peel.

3. Shred both celery roots with a hand grater and transfer to a serving bowl. Combine the lemon juice and mayonnaise. Pour over the celery root and toss.

## ◄ KITCHEN NOTES ►

- Add chickpeas and diced green apples.
- Serve the rémoulade as an appetizer, with other raw vegetables and vinaigrettes.
- It makes an excellent addition to sandwiches, like pulled pork.

# LEEKS IN VINAIGRETTE
## POIREAUX VINAIGRETTE

◆─◆

*Serves 2*

This dish can be served all year long, either warm or cold. The contrasting colors of the
sun-dried tomatoes and leeks make this a beautiful combination.

### ◆ INGREDIENTS ◆

- 4 leeks
- 2 teaspoons Dijon mustard
- 1 tablespoon red wine vinegar
- Salt and freshly ground pepper
- 2 tablespoons extra-virgin olive oil
- ½ cup arugula
- 6 sun-dried tomatoes

1. Gather your ingredients.

2. Remove the outside layers of the leeks and cut off the ends. Cut the leeks in half lengthwise and rinse.

3. Add to a pot of salted boiling water and cook for several minutes.

4. Remove the leeks from the water and plunge in an ice bath to stop the cooking. Drain on a paper towel.

5. Prepare your vinaigrette by combining the mustard, vinegar, salt, and pepper in a bowl and whisking until the mustard is dissolved. Add the olive oil and continue to whisk.

6. Arrange the leeks on a serving plate. Top with the arugula and sun-dried tomatoes. Drizzle generously with the vinaigrette and serve.

### ◆ KITCHEN NOTES ◆
- Serve with panfried fillet of sole for a healthy and simple meal.

*Salads*

# LENTIL SALAD

### SALADE DE LENTILLES

*Serves 4 to 6*

This makes an excellent side salad or appetizer, served warm or cold. Great served with cod or prawns and finished with a squeeze of lemon. Lentil salad is also a perfect accompaniment for warm duck or lamb confit.

## ‹ INGREDIENTS ›

- 1 carrot
- 1 cucumber
- 2 celery ribs
- 1 yellow bell pepper
- 1 red bell pepper
- ½ shallot
- ¼ cup fresh parsley leaves
- 1 tablespoon plus 1 teaspoon red wine vinegar
- 2 teaspoons balsamic vinegar
- ½ cup extra-virgin olive oil
- Salt and freshly ground pepper
- Cooked lentils (page 199)
- Sun-dried tomatoes for garnish

1. Gather your ingredients.

2. Peel the carrot. Chop the carrot, cucumber, celery, and bell peppers into a small dice and transfer to a large bowl. Chop the shallot and parsley and add to the bowl.

3. Prepare your vinaigrette by whisking together both vinegars, the olive oil, salt, and pepper. Add the lentils to the vegetables. Pour the vinaigrette over all and mix well, adding additional oil if needed.

## ‹ KITCHEN NOTES ›

- To simplify this recipe, combine just lentils, chopped onions, and vinaigrette.
- Add a little bit of pimento, if you dare.

# QUINOA & RATATOUILLE

## SALADE DE QUINOA ET RATATOUILLE

*Serves 8*

This is a refreshing and healthy salad from the South of France.
The combination is similar in style to a tabbouleh and is best served at room temperature.

### ◄ INGREDIENTS ►

- 2 zucchini
- 1 eggplant
- 1 red bell pepper
- 1 yellow bell pepper
- 1 onion
- 2 tomatoes
- 1 garlic clove
- 5 tablespoons extra-virgin olive oil
- 2 cups quinoa
- 4 cups water
- ½ cup fresh cilantro leaves
- ½ cup fresh parsley leaves
- 3 lemons
- Salt and freshly ground pepper

1. Gather your ingredients.

2. To make the ratatouille, finely dice the zucchini, eggplant, bell peppers, onion, and 1 of the tomatoes. Chop the garlic.

3. In a large sauté pan over medium heat, heat 3 tablespoons of the olive oil and sauté the onion and garlic for 2 minutes. Add the bell peppers and cook for another 2 minutes.

4. Add the eggplant and cook for an another 5 minutes. Finally, add the zucchini and cook for 8 more minutes. Remove from the heat, transfer to a plate, and refrigerate.

5. In a large saucepan over medium-high heat, heat the remaining 2 tablespoons of olive oil and add the quinoa. Reduce heat to low. Cook for 2 minutes. Add the water and cook for 8 to 10 minutes or until the water is absorbed. If the quinoa hasn't fully opened, add boiling water slowly and reduce.

6. Coarsely chop the cilantro and parsley and set aside. Peel the lemons entirely. Section the lemons, extract the meaty segments, and cut into pieces. Press what's left in your palm to juice.

7. Mix the ratatouille and quinoa in a large bowl.

8. Mix in the lemon juice and lemon sections.

9. Finely dice the remaining tomato and add to the bowl. Season with salt and pepper to taste.

# POTATO SALAD

## SALADE DE POMMES DE TERRE

*Serves 6*

This is a beautiful and delicious potato salad. Fantastic on its own or with smoked herring or salmon.

### INGREDIENTS

- 2 Yukon gold potatoes
- 4 red potatoes
- 2 shallots

- ½ cup fresh parsley leaves
- ½ cup fresh dill
- 3 tablespoons Champagne vinegar

- ¼ cup plus 2 tablespoons extra-virgin olive oil
- 3 tablespoons Dijon mustard

- Salt and freshly ground pepper

1. Gather your ingredients.

2. Cook the Yukon gold potatoes in one pot of salted boiling water and the red potatoes in another. Drain and let cool. Thinly slice the shallots.

3. Finely chop the parsley and dill.

4. Peel the Yukon gold potatoes but leave the skins on the red ones. Slice the potatoes and put in a bowl.

5. Whisk the vinegar, olive oil, and mustard and season with salt and pepper. Add the parsley and dill and mix.

6. Pour the vinaigrette over the potatoes and mix gently, being careful not to break them.

### KITCHEN NOTES

- This salad is great as an accompaniment to smoked fish.
- Warm the vinaigrette up for a few seconds in the microwave before mixing with the potatoes.
- Serve the potato salad with rye bread with caraway seeds.
- Fold in avocado wedges at the last minute.

# CAESAR SALAD
## SALADE CÉSAR

*Serves 2*

We had to include a Caesar salad because this is a staple menu item not only at La Boulange but also at most cafés in France.
This is our take on a classic. We use brioche croutons, which melt in your mouth, and Parmesan Crisps (page 198) for an extra crunch.
To vary the texture, use equal parts of kale and romaine lettuce.

### ⊰ INGREDIENTS ⊱

- Caesar Dressing (page 200)
- 2 Parmesan Crisps (page 198)
- 1 head romaine lettuce
- ¼ cup Croutons (page 196) made with brioche

1. Gather your ingredients. Prepare the Caesar dressing and Parmesan crisps first.

2. Cut the stem off the head of lettuce. Remove five outer leaves and place in a serving bowl.

3. Halve the remaining lettuce lengthwise. Cut one half crosswise into strips ½ inch wide. Cut the other half lengthwise into longer strips, for a variety of leaf lengths. Put in a mixing bowl.

4. Pour all but a few tablespoons of the Caesar dressing over the lettuce and toss thoroughly.

5. Transfer to the serving bowl.

6. Drizzle with additional dressing, and add the croutons and Parmesan crisps.

### ⊰ KITCHEN NOTES ⊱
- Add pieces of anchovy, grilled chicken, shrimp, or steak.

*Salads*

# WARM GOAT CHEESE SALAD

## SALADE DE CHÈVRE CHAUD

*Serves 4*

This has been a staple on the La Boulange menu since day one. The salad highlights a delicious combination of sharp goat cheese and candied pecans. Coat the goat cheese with bread crumbs and panfry just before you serve, to make sure you have warm, gooey balls.

### ⊰ INGREDIENTS ⊱

- 2 tablespoons chopped fresh Provençal herbs (¾ teaspoon each rosemary, dill, thyme, and chives)
- 11 ounces goat cheese
- 1 egg, beaten
- ½ cup bread crumbs
- 1 tablespoon extra-virgin olive oil
- 8 cups mixed greens
- ½ cup Balsamic Vinaigrette (page 199)
- 24 candied pecans
- 12 cherry tomatoes, cut in half
- 4 slices sourdough bread, toasted

1. Gather your ingredients.

2. In a bowl, mix the herbs with the goat cheese.

3. Using your hands, form the goat cheese into four small balls and refrigerate for at least 2 hours.

4. Dip the cheese balls in the egg wash.

5. On a baking sheet, spread out the bread crumbs and roll the cheese in the crumbs to cover.

6. In a medium skillet over medium heat, heat the olive oil and panfry the goat cheese until both sides are golden brown. Toss the greens with the dressing, and plate with pecans, tomatoes, and goat cheese. Serve with toasted bread.

### ⊰ KITCHEN NOTES ⊱

- You can use Brie instead of goat cheese.
- Drizzle with olive oil.

*Salads*

# NIÇOISE SALAD

SALADE NIÇOISE

*Serves 1*

This is a famous salad from the South of France. A true French classic. For a twist on the original, you can replace the tuna with salmon.

## ‹ INGREDIENTS ›

- 1 cup green beans
- 2 baby red potatoes or whatever you have on hand
- 1 red bell pepper
- 2 tomatoes
- 4 hard-boiled eggs
- Lettuce
- 20 anchovy fillets
- One 5-ounce can tuna packed in oil or water
- 12 olives
- ½ cup Balsamic Vinaigrette (page 199)
- Salt and freshly ground pepper

1. Gather your ingredients.

2. Cook the green beans and potatoes separately in salted boiling water until tender and drain. Peel the potatoes, slice ¼ inch thick, and set aside. Thinly slice the bell pepper, cut the tomatoes into wedges, and quarter the hard-boiled eggs.

3. Make a bed of the lettuce on a serving plate. Arrange the potatoes, bell peppers, tomatoes, and green beans on the lettuce. Add the eggs, anchovies, tuna, and olives and drizzle with the vinaigrette. Season with salt and pepper.

## ‹ KITCHEN NOTES ›

- If you're not an anchovy fan, replace them with cornichons or capers to keep a salty element.

# SMOKED TROUT SALAD
## SALADE DE TRUITE FUMÉE

*Serves 2*

This is one of our best-selling salads at La Boulange. The combination of apple, avocado, and smoked trout is wonderful.
We serve this salad with warm walnut croutons, which you can make at home.

### ⋅ INGREDIENTS ⋅

- 6 slices walnut or regular baguette
- ½ avocado
- 1 apple, such as a Braeburn
- 6 cherry tomatoes
- 5 ounces smoked trout fillet
- 4 cups mixed greens
- ¼ cup Lemon Vinaigrette (page 200)
- Salt and freshly ground pepper
- 2 lemon wedges

1. Gather your ingredients. Preheat the broiler.

2. Broil the baguette slices on a baking sheet for 5 minutes. Cut the avocado and apple into wedges and halve the cherry tomatoes. Cut the smoked trout fillet into pieces.

3. Toss the greens with the lemon vinaigrette in a bowl, and arrange on a serving plate. Add the avocado, apple, tomatoes, and trout pieces. Season with salt and pepper and serve with the lemon wedges and toasted baguette pieces.

### ⋅ KITCHEN NOTES ⋅

- Replace the lemon vinaigrette with warm, grainy mustard mixed with 2 tablespoons of lemon juice and 1 tablespoon of water.
- And, of course, you can substitute smoked salmon for the trout.

# SANDWICHES & TARTINES

# GRILLED CHEESE

### SANDWICH AUX TROIS FROMAGES

*Serves 1*

This is our twist on an American classic. We use mozzarella for texture and Swiss and blue cheeses for taste.
Serve this sandwich with tomato soup for the ultimate comfort meal. It's also great with a simple green salad or all by itself.

### ⊰ INGREDIENTS ⊱

- 1 slice Swiss cheese
- 2 slices country bread, toasted
- 1 ounce blue cheese, crumbled
- 2 slices mozzarella cheese

1. Gather your ingredients. Preheat the oven to 350°F.

2. Place the Swiss cheese over a slice of the toasted bread, follow with the blue cheese and the mozzarella cheese.

3. Cover with the remaining slice of bread and heat in the oven for a few minutes until the cheese is melted. Remove and press down with your hand.

### ⊰ KITCHEN NOTES ⊱

- Double the amount of blue cheese for a super-tasty and creamy version.
- Add a layer of thinly sliced pear between the cheeses.
- Eat with a little quince paste.
- For the ultimate cheesy experience, double the amount of cheese. After closing the sandwich, layer on the extra cheeses and top with a fried egg. Make sure to share this one!
- Sauteed button mushrooms work, as well.
- Serve with a green or quinoa salad for a more traditional side.

# GOAT CHEESE & PORTOBELLO MUSHROOM TARTINE

## TARTINE DE CHAMPIGNONS PORTOBELLO ET FROMAGE DE CHÈVRE

*Serves 1*

This tasty open-face sandwich is great for lunch, but also as an appetizer when cut into bite-size pieces.

### ‹ INGREDIENTS ›

- 2 portobello mushroom caps
- 2 tablespoons Dijon mustard
- 1 red bell pepper
- 1 tablespoon extra-virgin olive oil (optional)
- 2 tablespoons Pesto (page 204)
- 1 slice country bread
- 1 ounce goat cheese
- Salt and freshly ground pepper
- Arugula leaves for garnish

1. Gather your ingredients. Preheat the oven to 450°F.

2. Brush the mushroom caps on the inside with Dijon mustard and roast in the oven for 10 minutes, flipping after 5. Roast the bell pepper at the same time, brushing it with olive oil instead of mustard.

3. Set the mushrooms aside. Place the bell pepper in a bowl and cover with plastic wrap. The steam will help to loosen the skin. Wait 5 minutes and gently remove the skin.

4. Cut the roasted red pepper and mushroom caps into strips. Preheat the broiler.

5. Spread the pesto on the bread and cover with the mushrooms.

6. Layer the roasted pepper on top and add the goat cheese in dollops along the tartine. Season with salt and pepper. Broil for 2 minutes. Sprinkle with the arugula leaves.

### ‹ KITCHEN NOTES ›
- Serve with a side of Celery Rémoulade (page 51).

# SMOKED TURKEY & PROVOLONE TARTINE

## TARTINE A LA DINDE FUMÉE ET PROVOLONE

*Serves 1*

This is the French take on Thanksgiving—on a tartine. It was offered at the first La Boulange on Polk Street and it remains on the menu today, as it has consistently been a favorite of our customers. Remember this one for post-Thanksgiving leftovers.

### ◂ INGREDIENTS ▸

- 1 tablespoon Aioli (page 201)
- 1 slice country bread, toasted
- 4 or 5 slices smoked turkey breast
- 1 tomato, sliced
- 3 slices Provolone cheese

1. Gather your ingredients. Preheat the broiler.

2. Spread the aioli on the toasted bread. Layer on the smoked turkey and tomato.

3. Add the Provolone cheese and broil for a few minutes, until the cheese is melted.

### ◂ KITCHEN NOTES ▸

- Try this with horseradish or cranberry relish.

# SHAVED FENNEL & CELERY TARTINE

## TARTINE DE CÉLERI ET FENOUIL

*Serves 2*

This is a light, simple tartine. Don't hesitate to add basil or your favorite herbs or crumbled cheese.
It's a perfect appetizer for a summer gathering.

### ◄ INGREDIENTS ►

- ½ fennel bulb
- 1 bunch celery

- 3 asparagus tips
- 4 sun-dried tomatoes
- 4 kalamata olives, pitted

- 1 tablespoon Pistou (page 204)
- 4 slices baguette, toasted

- Extra-virgin olive oil for drizzling

1. Gather your ingredients.

2. Shave the fennel bulb and the thick base of the celery with a mandolin or a hand grater. (Store the celery ribs for another use.)

3. Thinly slice the asparagus tips lengthwise. Cut the sun-dried tomatoes into thirds and the olives into quarters.

4. Spread the pistou on the toasted baguette slices.

5. Layer the fennel and celery on the baguette slices.

6. Distribute the olives and sun-dried tomatoes evenly. Lay the asparagus on top, and drizzle with the olive oil.

# SARDINE TARTINE

### TARTINE DE SARDINE MÉDITERRANÉENNE

*Serves 2*

This is a favorite tartine of mine and my brother's. In France you can buy family-size cans of sardines (with twenty fillets), which we used to pick up along with a stick of butter and a baguette. We'd put it all together, sprinkle with a little salt and pepper, and eat the whole thing, just the two of us, in one sitting. Sardines are no joke in our family. This is our version of my childhood sardine sandwich.

## ◀ INGREDIENTS ▶

- 1 tomato
- ½ medium shallot
- 1 garlic clove
- 3 fresh basil leaves

- 5 olives, pitted
- 2 tablespoons extra-virgin olive oil

- 3 tablespoons balsamic vinegar
- ¼ baguette

- 3 to 5 sardine fillets
- Salt and freshly ground pepper

1. Gather your ingredients.

2. Thickly slice the tomato. Finely chop the shallot, garlic, and basil. Halve the olives.

3. In a large sauté pan over high heat, heat the olive oil and quickly sear the tomatoes on each side. Remove from the pan.

4. In the same pan, sauté the shallots and garlic for 1 minute, and then add the basil and olives and sauté for another minute. Making sure to keep the heat high, pour in the balsamic vinegar and deglaze for less than a minute, scraping up any browned bits.

5. Spoon some of the mixture on each tomato slice.

6. Cut the hunk of baguette in half and lay in the pan for a few minutes to absorb the juices and flavors. Place half of the tomato slices on the basted side of each baguette half and top with the sardine fillets. Cover with the remaining mixture and season with salt and pepper.

# CREAMY MUSHROOM TARTINE

## TARTINE DE CHAMPIGNONS À LA CRÈME

*Serves 2*

This is a rich, creamy, hearty tartine. It started as a creamy mushroom crêpe, which we served at Galette,
our restaurant located in what is now La Boulange de Fillmore. We had many requests for this after Galette's time,
so we made it a tartine at La Boulange. It will surely warm you up on a cold day.

### ‹ INGREDIENTS ›

- ½ red onion
- 5 ounces button mushrooms
- 11 ounces cooked chicken
- 2 tablespoons extra-virgin olive oil
- 1 tablespoon all-purpose flour
- 1 tablespoon Dijon mustard
- 1 cup heavy cream
- Salt and freshly ground pepper
- 2 slices country bread

1. Gather your ingredients. Preheat the broiler.

2. Thinly slice the onion. Clean the mushrooms and trim the stems. Quarter and thinly slice. Cube the chicken.

3. In a large sauté pan over high heat, heat the olive oil and cook the onions until soft and translucent. Add the mushrooms, sauté for 5 minutes, and sprinkle with the flour.

4. Add the mustard and stir.

5. Add the cream and cook, stirring, until the cream is warmed through.

6. Add the chicken cubes and cook, stirring, for another few minutes. Season with salt and pepper to taste. Arrange on the bread and broil for 2 minutes to finish.

*Sandwiches & Tartines*

# TUNA MELT

## TARTINE DE SALADE DE THON

*Serves 2*

This one is all about the tuna mix. Our tuna salad includes apple and parsley, for a little crunch and color.

### ⊰ INGREDIENTS ⊱

- 1 green apple
- ¼ medium shallot
- 1 sprig fresh parsley
- One 5-ounce can tuna packed in oil or water
- 3 tablespoons Mayonnaise (page 201) or store-bought
- 1 slice country bread, toasted
- 1 tomato, sliced
- 3 slices cheddar cheese

1. Gather your ingredients. Preheat the broiler to 400°F.

2. Peel and dice the apple, finely dice the shallot, and mince the parsley leaves. In a bowl, combine the tuna, apple, shallot, and parsley. Add the mayonnaise and mix well.

3. Spread the tuna salad on the bread. Lay the tomato slices on top, and then the cheddar cheese. Broil for 3 to 4 minutes or until the cheese is melted. Cut in half before serving.

### ⊰ KITCHEN NOTES ⊱

- If you're looking for a healthy option, use a dollop of nonfat Greek yogurt instead of the mayonnaise.
- You can also use just 1 slice of cheese, broken up and spread evenly across the tuna.

# FLANK STEAK TARTINE

## TARTINE DE BAVETTE AUX OIGNONS

*Serves 1*

The creamy mushroom sauce and the caramelized onions really set this tartine apart. This one could be a game changer,
so if you want to splurge, go for a filet mignon. After you cook your meat, make sure to let it rest for a few minutes before cutting.
Don't be shy with the mushroom sauce and black pepper.

### ⋆ INGREDIENTS ⋆

- 2 tablespoons Mushroom Sauce (page 207)
- 2 tablespoons Caramelized Onions (page 195)
- 1 slice country bread, toasted
- 1 medium tomato, sliced
- ¼ cup extra-virgin olive oil, or 4 tablespoons butter
- 5 ounces flank steak, cut on the diagonal into ¼-inch-thick slices
- Salt and freshly ground pepper
- ½ cup arugula

1. Gather your ingredients.

2. Spread the mushroom sauce and caramelized onions generously on the toasted bread.

3. Layer the tomato slices on top. Set aside.

4. In a sauté pan over high heat, heat the olive oil or melt the butter and cook the flank steak a few minutes on each side. They should be slightly pink in the center. Season with salt and pepper.

5. Cut the steak slices on the diagonal into about four pieces per slice.

6. Layer the steak on top of the tomatoes, and season with salt and pepper. Scatter the arugula leaves on top.

### ⋆ KITCHEN NOTES ⋆

- Rib-eye would work and, if you have the cash, a filet mignon would surely be delicious!

*Sandwiches & Tartines*

# LA BOULANGE CLUB

*Serves 1*

In the great tradition of club sandwiches, this is our take. Eat it with fries, Tabasco, and ketchup.

### ◄ INGREDIENTS ►

- 2 tablespoons Aioli (page 201)
- 2 slices bacon
- 3 slices *pain de mie* or white sandwich bread
- 3 slices turkey breast
- ½ cup chopped butter lettuce
- 4 slices tomato
- ½ avocado, sliced

1. Gather your ingredients. Prepare your aioli and cook the bacon slices until crisp.

2. Toast the *pain de mie*. Spread the aioli on one slice. Roll up each turkey slice and lay the rolls over the aioli. Top with the chopped lettuce. Spread another slice of bread with aioli on both sides and place on the lettuce.

3. Add the bacon, sliced tomato, and avocado. Spread aioli on one side of the third slice of bread, and close the sandwich.

### ◄ KITCHEN NOTES ►
- This sandwich is great made with toasted brioche.

# PROVENÇAL BLT

*Serves 1*

Although this is one of our simple sandwiches, if you use great bread, great bacon, and a great tomato, it's one of the best. Our twist is the goat cheese and aioli. To really make this sandwich sing, double the amount of bacon and goat cheese; we think it will be quite worthwhile.

## ⊰ INGREDIENTS ⊱

- 2 slices bacon
- 1 ciabatta roll
- 2 tablespoons Aioli (page 201)

- 1 tomato, sliced
- 1 ounce goat cheese
- 2 leaves lettuce

1. Gather your ingredients.

2. Cook the bacon until crisp and set aside. Halve the ciabatta roll and spread the aioli on the cut sides of the roll. Layer the tomato on the bottom of the roll and top with the goat cheese.

3. Add the bacon and lettuce, and cover with the top of the roll.

## ⊰ KITCHEN NOTES ⊱
- Use arugula instead of lettuce for a bite.

# PORTOBELLO BURGER

*Serves 1*

This proud vegetarian alter ego of our Boulange burger is just as good. Great with a little quinoa salad or the usual fries.

## ◦ INGREDIENTS ◦

- 1 portobello mushroom cap
- 1 tablespoon Dijon mustard

- 1½ ounces Brie cheese (2 slices)
- 1 tablespoon Aioli (page 201)

- 1 sandwich or burger bun
- 3 slices tomato
- 1 tablespoon Balsamic Vinaigrette (page 199)

- ¼ cup arugula leaves

1. Gather your ingredients. Preheat the oven to 400°F.

2. Brush the inside of the mushroom cap with the mustard and place on a baking sheet. Roast for 10 minutes.

3. Preheat the broiler and broil the slices of Brie on the mushroom cap in an oven-safe dish or pan for 1 minute.

4. Halve the bun and spread the aioli on the cut sides of the bun. Place the mushroom cap on the bottom half, and layer the tomato on top.

5. Drizzle with some of the vinaigrette. Add the arugula, drizzle with the remaining vinaigrette, and close the sandwich.

# LA BOULANGE BURGER

*Serves 1*

Just try this—trust us. For a cheeseburger, use blue cheese or sharp cheddar.

### ◄ INGREDIENTS ►

- 6 ounces ground beef
- 1 teaspoon unsalted butter (optional)
- 1 tablespoon Aioli (page 201)
- 1 burger bun, toasted
- 1 tablespoon Caramelized Onions (page 195)
- 2 tomato slices
- 2 lettuce leaves

1. Gather your ingredients. Form the beef into a patty.

2. Heat a nonstick skillet over high heat. Cook the burger patty for 2 to 3 minutes on each side for medium-rare. To caramelize the burger, add the bit of butter at the end.

3. Spread the aioli on the top and bottom halves of the bun. Place the burger on the bun and top with the caramelized onions, tomato, and lettuce. Close the sandwich.

### ◄ KITCHEN NOTES ►

- Add a fried egg or a few slices of avocado.

# LOBSTER SANDWICH

### SANDWICH DE HOMARD

*Serves 1*

Have you ever had a croissant bun? Other than the ones we make for La Boulange, you can't find them anywhere, so it's not really a fair question, and this photo is a bit of a tease. A brioche bun, any kind of soft burger bun, or the traditional hot dog roll works well with this sandwich.

## ◄ INGREDIENTS ►

- ⅓ celery rib
- 2 sprigs fresh tarragon
- 1 teaspoon grated lemon zest, plus 1 teaspoon juice
- 1 tablespoon Aioli (page 201)

- ¼ cup Celery Rémoulade (page 51)
- 1 croissant bun or any soft bun, toasted
- About ¼ pound cooked lobster

1. Gather your ingredients.

2. Finely chop the celery and tarragon leaves.

3. Mix together the celery, lemon zest and juice, tarragon, aioli, and celery rémoulade. Spread the celery mix on the bottom half of the bun, and then add the lobster. Cover it with the top of the bun.

## ◄ KITCHEN NOTES ►

- For a fraction of the price, you can use faux lobster, and it's still really good.

# SPRING TARTINE
## TARTINE DE PRINTEMPS

*Serves 1*

This tartine is quite an unusual and interesting combination of spring vegetables.
Each vegetable is prepared separately, so this takes a little time, but it is well worth it.

### ⊰ INGREDIENTS ⊱

- ¼ cup pearl onions
- ½ tablespoon butter
- 1 tablespoon sugar

- 3 stems Swiss chard
- Juice of 1 lemon
- 2 tablespoons flour

- 5 asparagus stalks
- ¼ cup fresh shelled fava beans

- 1 teaspoon extra-virgin olive oil
- ¼ cup artichoke hearts

- 1 tablespoon Persillade (page 196)

- Salt and freshly ground pepper
- 1 slice country bread

1. Gather your ingredients.

2. In a saucepan over high heat, combine the onions with enough water to almost cover. Add ¼ tablespoon butter and sugar. Bring to a boil, reduce the heat to medium, and cook until the water evaporates and the onions are caramelized.

3. Rinse and stem the chard. Set aside the leaves. Cut the stems into 1-inch pieces and combine in a saucepan with lemon juice, flour, and enough water to cover the chard stems. Boil until tender and plunge the stems into an ice bath.

4. Boil the asparagus in a pot of salted boiling water for 5 to 7 minutes. Add the fava beans and cook for 1 more minute. Drain and plunge into an ice bath. Skin the fava beans.

5. Bundle and chop the chard leaves. Cut the asparagus stems into small pieces, cut the tips in half lengthwise, and cook in a pot of salted boiling water.

6. In a large skillet over high heat, heat the olive oil and cook the chard leaves for about 2 minutes and remove from the pan.

7. In the same pan, heat the chard stems, caramelized onions, and artichoke quarters for a minute or two, stirring.

8. Add the remaining butter, fava beans, asparagus, persillade, and chard leaves and sauté for just a minute or two to combine. Season with salt and pepper.

9. Arrange everything on the toasted bread.

# SUMMER TARTINE

## TARTINE D'ÉTÉ

*Serves 1*

Once your eggplant caviar is made, use it as much as you can because it's absolutely delicious, especially when combined with ripe tomatoes, fresh basil, and goat cheese or burrata.

### ◂ INGREDIENTS ▸

- 1 tomato
- 2½ ounces goat cheese or burrata
- 3 fresh basil leaves
- 3 tablespoons Eggplant Caviar (page 197)
- 1 slice country bread
- Salt and freshly ground pepper
- Extra-virgin olive oil for drizzling (optional)

1. Gather your ingredients. Preheat the broiler.

2. Slice the tomato and goat cheese. Thinly slice the basil leaves.

3. Spread a thick layer of eggplant caviar on the bread and layer the tomato and cheese on top. Broil for 2 to 3 minutes. Sprinkle with the basil and add salt and pepper to taste. Drizzle with the olive oil, if desired.

# AUTUMN TARTINE
## TARTINE D'AUTOMNE

*Serves 1*

You don't need to wait until autumn to make this tartine; it's wonderful anytime. The topping is quite simple to make and can be used as a side for any main course. An interesting mix of mushrooms can really liven up this basic tartine, so don't be shy when you're selecting.

### ◀ INGREDIENTS ▶

- 6 ounces butternut squash, peeled
- ½ small shallot
- 6 ounces mixed white button and wild mushrooms
- 2 teaspoons extra-virgin olive oil
- 3 sprigs fresh thyme
- ½ tablespoon unsalted butter
- 1 tablespoon Persillade (page 196)
- Salt and freshly ground pepper
- 1 slice country bread, toasted

1. Gather your ingredients.

2. Peel, seed, and dice the butternut squash. Finely dice the shallot.

3. Clean the mushrooms. Slice the white mushrooms and remove the stems from the wild ones.

4. In a skillet over high heat, heat 1 teaspoon of the olive oil and sauté the squash for 2 to 3 minutes. Add the thyme. Cover, lower the heat to medium, and cook for about 10 minutes, stirring occasionally. Set aside.

5. In another skillet, heat the remaining 1 teaspoon of olive oil, and sauté the mushrooms over medium heat for a few minutes until tender.

6. Add the mushrooms, butter, persillade, and shallot to the squash and mix. Season with salt and pepper. Arrange on the toasted bread.

# WINTER TARTINE
## TARTINE D'HIVER

*Serves 1*

For the root vegetable lover in you, this tartine is hearty, simple, and satisfying. If you have leftovers,
the cooked vegetable mix is wonderful eaten by itself or with a little melted Gruyère on top.

### ◂ INGREDIENTS ▸

- ½ turnip
- ½ parsnip
- ¼ celery root
- 1 carrot

- ¼ shallot
- 2 tablespoons extra-virgin olive oil
- 2 sprigs fresh thyme

- 1 teaspoon unsalted butter
- 1 tablespoon Persillade (page 196)
- Salt and freshly ground pepper

- 1 slice country bread, toasted
- Arugula leaves for garnish

1. Gather your ingredients.

2. Peel the turnip, parsnip, celery root, and carrot and cut into ½-inch pieces. Finely chop the shallot.

3. In a large skillet over medium-high heat, heat the olive oil and sauté the vegetables until slightly colored.

4. Add the thyme, cover, and reduce the heat to medium. Cook for several minutes more until tender.

5. Uncover and remove the thyme. Add the butter and shallot and sauté for 1 minute. Add the persillade, stir, and season with salt and pepper.

6. Arrange the vegetable mix on the toasted bread. Finish with the arugula.

### ◂ KITCHEN NOTES ▸
- Use any kind of root vegetable, including daikon, sweet potato, or rutabaga.

# BLOOD SAUSAGE TARTINE

## TARTINE DE BOUDIN NOIR

*Serves 4*

Wow!

### ⊰ INGREDIENTS ⊱

- 1 apple
- 2 blood sausages
- 1 tablespoon unsalted butter
- Salt and freshly ground pepper
- 2 slices country bread, toasted
- Arugula leaves for garnish

1. Gather your ingredients.

2. Peel and core the apple and cut into wedges. Cut the blood sausages on the diagonal into ¼-inch slices. In a skillet, melt ½ tablespoon of the butter over medium-high heat, and brown the apple wedges.

3. Remove the apples and set aside. Add the blood sausages to the pan. Cook for 1 to 2 minutes on each side over medium-high heat. Remove from the pan and set aside.

4. Add the remaining ½ tablespoon of butter, a dash of water, salt, and pepper to the pan, and stir to loosen the browned bits of sausage. Reduce for a minute or two.

5. Lay both sides of the bread in the skillet to absorb the cooking juices.

6. Arrange the apple and sausages on the bread. Scatter the arugula on top.

### ⊰ KITCHEN NOTES ⊱

- Wow!

# SAVORY TARTS, FEUILLETÉS, QUICHES & GRATINS

# ZUCCHINI TART

### TARTE AUX DEUX COURGETTES

*Serves 4 to 6*

In this tart from the South of France, the béchamel sauce under the vegetables gives it a wonderful smooth and creamy texture. Excellent served with a simple green salad.

## ◄ INGREDIENTS ►

- 2 small zucchini
- 4 small yellow squash
- ¼ red onion
- 2 garlic cloves

- 1 tablespoon fresh thyme leaves
- 1 tablespoon extra-virgin olive oil
- Salt and freshly ground pepper

- Savory Shortcrust Dough (page 192) or store-bought
- ½ cup Béchamel Sauce (page 203)
- 12 to 15 cherry tomatoes, halved

- ⅓ cup goat cheese
- Chopped fresh parsley for garnish

1. Gather your ingredients. Have a 13¾-by-4½-inch rectangular tart pan ready. Preheat the oven to 400°F.

2. Slice the zucchini and yellow squash on the diagonal. Slice the onion and cut into 2-inch pieces. Finely chop the garlic and thyme. In a large sauté pan over medium-high heat, heat the olive oil and sauté the zucchini, yellow squash, onion, garlic, and thyme for 5 to 7 minutes or until tender. Season with salt and pepper.

3. Roll out the dough so that it is slightly larger than your tart pan. Place the rolled-out dough in the pan. Spread the béchamel generously on the bottom of the tart shell. Fill with the zucchini mixture. Bake for 20 minutes. Add the cherry tomatoes, and bake for another 10 minutes. Finish with dollops of goat cheese and sprinkle with parsley.

## ◄ KITCHEN NOTES ►

- Replace the béchamel with tomato sauce.

# POTATO, GREEN ONION & BACON TART

### TARTE AUX POMMES DE TERRE

*Serves 4 to 6*

This tart is delicious because of the combination of flavors and the wonderful infusion of bacon juices in the potatoes.
Serve this warm with mixed greens for a great lunch or dinner.

## ◄ INGREDIENTS ►

- 1 pound Yukon gold potatoes
- Salt and freshly ground pepper
- ¼ cup extra-virgin olive oil
- 3 slices bacon
- 2 sprigs fresh parsley
- 1 sprig fresh rosemary
- ⅓ cup sliced green onion
- 3 ounces Swiss cheese, grated
- Savory Shortcrust Dough (page 192) or store-bought
- About ¾ cup heavy cream

1. Gather your ingredients. Have four individual tart pans or one 11-inch tart pan with a removable bottom ready. Preheat the oven to 400°F.

2. Peel the potatoes and slice about ¼ inch thick.

3. In a large baking pan, layer the potatoes and drizzle with the olive oil. Sprinkle with salt and pepper. Lay the bacon slices over the potatoes. Bake for 20 for 25 minutes.

4. Chop the parsley and rosemary leaves.

5. Remove the potatoes from the oven. The bacon slices will be slightly crispy, and the potatoes will be soft.

6. Cut the bacon into large chunks.

7. In a large bowl, combine the potatoes, green onion, parsley, rosemary, and bacon.

8. Add the Swiss cheese and mix well. Divide the dough into four if making individual tarts. Roll out so that the dough is slightly larger than each tart pan or the baking dish and transfer to the pans or dish.

9. Add the potato mixture and pour in enough cream to fill the pans or dish halfway. Bake for 15 to 20 minutes until the cheese is fully melted and it is golden brown on top.

# BAKER'S PIZZA

## PIZZA DU BOULANGER

*Serves 4*

In France, *boulangères* often make pizza using short pastry dough instead of yeasted dough. As long as you have the short dough made in advance and in your freezer (something everyone should do!), this type of pizza is very simple to make. All you need is a green salad served alongside for a perfect lunch or light dinner.

### ◄ INGREDIENTS ►

- Savory Shortcrust Dough (page 192) or store-bought
- 1 tomato
- ¾ cup Tomato Sauce (page 202) or store-bought
- ½ cup shredded Swiss cheese
- ¼ cup pitted black olives, halved
- 2 teaspoons chopped fresh thyme
- 6 to 8 anchovy fillets
- Extra-virgin olive oil for drizzling

1. Gather your ingredients. Have a 9- to 11-inch tart pan with a removable bottom ready. Preheat the oven to 375°F.

2. Roll out the dough so that it is slightly larger than the diameter of your tart pan.

3. Thinly slice the tomato.

4. Spread the tomato sauce over the dough and place a layer of sliced tomato to cover.

5. Sprinkle the Swiss cheese over the tomato and sauce, and then top with the olives, thyme, and anchovy fillets.

6. Bake the pizza for 30 minutes, or until the crust and cheese are golden brown. Drizzle with olive oil just before serving.

### ◄ KITCHEN NOTES ►

- Add cooked diced bacon, cooked crumbled sausage, or your favorite ham to the pizza before baking.
- Use your favorite vegetables, such as roasted red peppers, sautéed fennel, or sliced onions.
- Garnish the baked pizza with a handful of arugula leaves.
- Top the baked pizza with a fried egg.

*Savory Tarts, Feuilletés, Quiches & Gratins*

# PISSALADIÈRE

*Serves 8*

This Provençal staple will please anchovy lovers everywhere. If you're not an anchovy lover, feel free to leave them off; the olives and onions are still a great combination. Best served warm, with a glass of rosé.

## ◄ INGREDIENTS ►

- 4 onions
- 2 tablespoons extra-virgin olive oil

- 2 tablespoons sugar
- 1 tablespoon Herbes de Provence

- Savory Shortcrust Dough (page 192) or store-bought
- Two 2-ounce cans anchovy fillets, rinsed in cold water

- 10 kalamata olives, halved and pitted

1. Gather your ingredients. Have a 9- to 11-inch tart pan with a removable bottom ready. Preheat the oven to 400°F.

2. Thinly slice the onions. In a large pot or skillet over medium-high heat, sweat (cook down) the onions in the olive oil until soft. Reduce the heat to medium and add the sugar and Herbes de Provence. Continue to cook until the onions are brown, stirring occasionally, about 30 minutes.

3. Roll out the dough so that it is slightly larger than your tart pan and lay it in the pan, crimping the edge so it's about ½ inch taller than the pan.

4. Spread out the onions evenly on the bottom of the crust.

5. Arrange the anchovies evenly across the onions.

6. Scatter the olives evenly among the anchovy fillets. Bake for 35 minutes.

*Savory Tarts, Feuilletés, Quiches & Gratins*

# QUICHE LORRAINE

*Serves 6 to 8*

This is a must-have in a French café cookbook, so here's our take. For the ultimate quiche Lorraine,
we added heavy cream instead of the traditional crème fraîche and include both prosciutto and baked ham.

## ⊰ INGREDIENTS ⊱

- Savory Shortcrust Dough
  (page 192) or store-bought
- 5 ounces baked ham
- 5 ounces prosciutto
- 1 cup milk
- 1 cup heavy cream
- 2 eggs
- ½ teaspoon salt
- ¼ teaspoon freshly ground
  pepper
- 5 ounces Gruyère cheese,
  grated

1. Gather your ingredients. Have a 9- to 11-inch tart pan
with a removable bottom ready. Preheat the oven to 400°F.

2. Roll out the dough so that it is slightly larger than
your tart pan, transfer to the pan, and add the ham and
prosciutto. Mix the milk, cream, eggs, salt, and pepper in
a bowl and pour into the tart shell, covering the ham and
leaving about ¼ inch of crust exposed.

3. Sprinkle with the Gruyère cheese. Bake for 40 to
45 minutes, or until the custard is set and golden brown.

## ⊰ KITCHEN NOTES ⊱

- It's important to use a tart pan with a removable bottom, otherwise the liquid will not solidify.
Anna, sorry you found out the hard way . . . twice!

# QUICHE WITH SALMON & DILL

## QUICHE AU SAUMON ET A L'ANETH

*Serves 6 to 8*

This is a variation on a classic quiche, terrific for a summertime brunch or lunch.

### ◦ INGREDIENTS ◦

- 5 to 7 ounces frozen spinach (without water)
- Savory Shortcrust Dough (page 192) or store-bought
- 1 or 2 sprigs fresh dill
- ¾ pound salmon fillet, cubed
- 1 cup milk
- 1 cup heavy cream
- 2 eggs
- 2 teaspoons salt
- 3 teaspoons freshly ground pepper
- ¾ cup grated Swiss cheese

1. Gather your ingredients. Have an 11-inch tart pan with a removable bottom ready. Preheat the oven to 400°F.

2. Thaw and drain the frozen spinach. Roll out the dough so that it is slightly larger than your tart pan and transfer to the pan. Mix the spinach and dill together in a bowl and lay in the bottom of the tart shell. Add the chunks of salmon.

3. Mix the milk, cream, eggs, salt, and pepper in a bowl. Pour over the salmon and spinach, leaving about ¼ inch of crust exposed. Sprinkle with the Swiss cheese. Bake for 40 minutes or until the custard is set and golden brown.

*Savory Tarts, Feuilletés, Quiches & Gratins*

# BRIE & BACON FEUILLETÉ

## FEUILLETTÉ AU BACON ET AU BRIE

*Serves 2*

This is our own version of Brie *en croûte*. A *feuilleté* is a puff pastry pocket. We've added mozzarella and bacon. Simple and delicious.

### ◄ INGREDIENTS ►

- 4 puff pastry squares, about 5 to 6 inches
- ¼ pound Brie cheese
- 3 ounces mozzarella cheese, grated
- 4 slices bacon
- Freshly ground pepper
- 1 egg, beaten

1. Gather your ingredients. Have a baking sheet ready. Preheat the oven to 400°F.

2. Lay the puff pastry squares on a floured surface. Slice the Brie. Divide the cheeses evenly between two pastry squares, placing them in the center of each one. Lay 2 slices of bacon over the cheeses. Season with pepper.

3. Cover each filled square with an unfilled one. Brush with the egg wash and score the top with the tip of a knife. Place on the baking sheet and bake for 22 to 25 minutes or until golden brown.

### ◄ KITCHEN NOTES ►

- You can add sautéed mushrooms to the puff squares.
- Replace the bacon with a dollop of jam, for a sweet and cheesy treat.

# WILD MUSHROOM MACARONI & CHEESE

## GRATIN DE MACARONI AUX CHAMPIGNONS

*Serves 2*

This is our adult version of macaroni and cheese, where wild mushrooms, cayenne pepper, three cheeses, and béchamel meet. Rich, creamy, and delicious.

### ◄ INGREDIENTS ►

- 7 ounces mixed wild mushrooms
- 1 tablespoon extra-virgin olive oil
- 5 ounces macaroni
- 1 cup Béchamel Sauce (page 203)
- 1 ounce white Cheddar, shredded
- 1 ounce Jack cheese, shredded
- 1 teaspoon cayenne pepper
- 1 ounce shredded Swiss cheese
- Salt and freshly ground pepper

1. Gather your ingredients. Have two 8-by-5-inch baking dishes ready. Preheat the broiler.

2. Clean the mushrooms and remove the stems. In a medium skillet over medium-high heat, sauté the mushrooms in the olive oil until soft. Cook the macaroni in a pot of salted boiling water until al dente.

3. In a medium saucepan over medium heat, mix the béchamel with the Cheddar and Jack cheeses. Cook, stirring, until the cheeses are melted. Add the cayenne, mushrooms, and macaroni. Divide between two baking dishes, and sprinkle with the Swiss cheese. Broil for 2 to 3 minutes or until the cheese is browned and a little crispy. Season with salt and pepper.

### ◄ KITCHEN NOTES ►

- Drizzle with truffle or spicy oil just before serving.

# GRATIN DAUPHINOIS

### Serves 6

This potato dish is creamy, creamy, creamy. Excellent with roast pork or beef.

## ⁌ INGREDIENTS ⁌

- 4 cups milk
- 3 sprigs fresh thyme
- 3 bay leaves
- 4 or 5 garlic cloves
- 7 Yukon gold potatoes
- Salt and freshly ground pepper
- 2 cups heavy cream

1. Gather your ingredients. Have a 10-by-14-inch baking dish with 2-inch sides ready. Preheat the oven to 350°F.

2. In a large pot, combine the milk, thyme, bay leaves, and garlic. Bring to a boil.

3. Peel the potatoes and slice them about ¼ inch thick. For a shorter cooking time, slice the potatoes thinner.

4. Poach the potatoes in the hot milk mixture for 3 to 4 minutes. They should be slightly firm. Remove with a slotted spoon, reserving the milk. Turn milk mixture to low heat. Layer the potatoes in the baking dish.

5. Add salt and pepper to the cream and pour over the potatoes.

6. Pour enough of the reserved milk over the potatoes to cover them. Discard the rest. Bake the potatoes for about 45 minutes or until golden brown.

## ⁌ KITCHEN NOTES ⁌
- For a lighter version, replace 1 cup of the cream with an additional 1 cup of hot milk.

*Savory Tarts, Feuilletés, Quiches & Gratins*

# WINTER VEGETABLE GRATIN

## GRATIN DE RACINES D'HIVER

*Serves 2*

This is one of our most successful winter specials at La Boulange.
It can be made ahead of time and finished with the Swiss cheese just before serving.

### ◄ INGREDIENTS ►

- 1 Yukon gold potato
- 1 carrot
- ½ celery root
- 1 turnip
- ½ parsnip

- 1 teaspoon extra-virgin olive oil
- 1 tablespoon Persillade (page 196)
- 1 ounce Swiss cheese, shredded

1. Gather your ingredients. Have an ovenproof bowl about 7 inches in diameter ready. Preheat the broiler.

2. Peel and thinly slice the potato, carrot, celery root, turnip, and parsnip.

3. In a large sauté pan over high heat, sauté the vegetables in the olive oil for 5 minutes. Reduce the heat to medium and sauté for another 15 minutes or until tender. Stir in the persillade. Pour the mix into a baking dish and sprinkle with the Swiss cheese. Broil for 2 to 3 minutes.

### ◄ KITCHEN NOTES ►

• Use Parmesan or Gruyère instead of Swiss cheese.

• All root vegetables work well in this dish; use what's on hand or easily found in your local market.

# BOULANGE POTATOES
## POMMES BOULANGÈRES

*Serves 6*

The name *pommes boulangères* comes from the tradition of French villagers bringing their potatoes to the baker, or *boulanger*, to cook in the bread ovens. Before the time when all homes had an oven, the baker was essential not only for his bread but also for his oven. This is a popular side at La Boulange and a wonderful dish to serve with roasted pork, lamb, or chicken. The thinly sliced potatoes makes this simple presentation beautiful.

### ⊰ INGREDIENTS ⊱

- 2 medium onions
- 3 tablespoons extra-virgin olive oil
- 4 pounds Yukon gold potatoes
- 3 slices bacon
- 3 sprigs fresh thyme
- 3 bay leaves
- 5 garlic cloves
- ½ cup white wine
- 2 to 3 cups chicken broth or water
- Salt and freshly ground pepper

1. Gather your ingredients. Have a 10-by-14-inch baking dish with 2-inch sides ready. Preheat the oven to 400°F.

2. Peel and thinly slice the onions. In a large sauté pan over medium heat, cook the onions in the olive oil until soft and translucent.

3. Peel the potatoes and cut in half lengthwise. Thinly slice crosswise, maintaining the shape of the potato.

4. Layer the onions in the bottom of the baking dish and place the bacon on top.

5. Arrange the sliced potatoes on top of the bacon. Put the thyme, bay leaves, and whole garlic cloves in the crevices.

6. Combine the white wine and chicken broth in a bowl and ladle over the potatoes to cover. Bake for 1 hour. Add salt and pepper to taste and serve.

### ⊰ KITCHEN NOTES ⊱

- This is a great accompaniment for meat, fish, or vegetables. It's also an excellent brunch dish.

*Savory Tarts, Feuilletés, Quiches & Gratins*

# MAIN DISHES, MONTHLY SPECIALS & LA BOULANGE FRIDAYS

# PENNE WITH VEGETABLES

## PENNE AUX LÉGUMES

*Serves 2*

Simple and healthy, this is a great weeknight dinner dish. It keeps well, so you can enjoy the leftovers.

### ◄ INGREDIENTS ►

- 1 small carrot
- 1 small zucchini
- 1 small shallot
- 9 button mushrooms

- 6 ounces penne
- 10 green beans
- 1 teaspoon extra-virgin olive oil, plus more for finishing

- 8 artichoke hearts, quartered
- 2 tablespoons Persillade (page 196)

- Salt and freshly ground pepper

1. Gather your ingredients.

2. Peel the carrot. Slice the carrot and zucchini on the diagonal. Finely dice the shallot, and quarter the mushrooms. Cook the penne in a pot of salted boiling water, drain, and transfer to a large bowl.

3. Cook the green beans in saucepan of salted boiling water for 2 to 3 minutes, making sure they are still a little crunchy. Drain and cut in half.

4. In a medium sauté pan over high heat, heat the olive oil and sauté the carrot, zucchini, mushrooms, and artichokes for 5 minutes. Reduce to medium heat until the veggies are just tender.

5. Add the persillade and sauté for 1 to 2 minutes.

6. Finally, add the shallot and sauté briefly. Combine all the vegetables with the penne and toss. Add salt and pepper to taste and finish with olive oil if needed.

# FARRO RISOTTO

## RISOTTO D'ÉPEAUTRE

*Serves 4 to 6*

There is nothing more comforting than this risotto. It is very rich, so a small serving goes a long way.
Farro, a delicious, healthy, and chewy ancient grain, makes a wonderful accompaniment to meat or fish and vegetables.

### ⟨ INGREDIENTS ⟩

- 2 tablespoons extra-virgin olive oil
- 2 cups farro

- ¼ cup white wine
- About 4 cups chicken broth

- ¾ cup heavy cream
- 2 medium shallots

- 4 or 5 green onions
- ½ cup grated Parmesan cheese

- 4 tablespoons unsalted butter

- Salt and freshly ground pepper

1. Gather your ingredients.

2. In a large pot over medium-high heat, heat the olive oil and add the farro. Cook, stirring, for 1 to 2 minutes.

3. Add the wine and cook for 3 minutes. Add enough chicken broth so that it just covers the farro and simmer for 30 minutes, adding more broth as needed to keep the liquid at the same level.

4. Simmer for about 15 minutes more, until the farro is tender and chewy and all or most of the liquid has been absorbed. In a medium bowl, whisk the cream until thickened.

5. Finely dice the shallots and set aside.

6. Finely chop the green onions and set aside.

7. Return the farro to medium heat and add the Parmesan cheese and butter.

8. Add the cream and mix well.

9. Finally, add the green onions and shallots and give the risotto a few stirs. Season with salt and pepper.

# SHRIMP PERSILLADE

## CREVETTES EN PERSILLADE

---

*Serves 4*

We prepare this rice dish as a pilaf, with a simple sautéed shrimp, parsley, and garlic sauce. I could eat it every day.

### ◦ INGREDIENTS ◦

- ½ medium onion
- 2 tablespoons extra-virgin olive oil
- 1½ cups rice

- 2¼ cups water
- 15 medium or large shrimp, peeled with tails left on

- 2 tablespoons Persillade (page 196)
- 1 tablespoon unsalted butter

- Salt and freshly ground pepper

1. Gather your ingredients.

2. Finely dice the onion.

3. In a large saucepan over medium heat, heat 1 tablespoon of the olive oil and sauté the onions until translucent.

4. Add the rice and stir. Add the water. Bring to a boil, reduce the heat to low, and cook, covered, until the water is absorbed, about 15 to 20 minutes. Remove from the heat.

5. In a sauté pan over high heat, heat the remaining 1 tablespoon of olive oil and cook the shrimp for about 1 minute on each side.

6. Add the persillade and butter. Sauté for 1 to 2 minutes. Season with salt and pepper.

### ◦ KITCHEN NOTES ◦

- Instead of persillade, use ground chipotle chile or coconut milk and curry powder.

# TILAPIA WITH WHITE BEANS
## TILAPIA AUX HARICOTS BLANCS

*Serves 4*

The acidity of the balsamic vinegar and the spiciness of the chorizo are wonderful complements to the white beans.
Tilapia is a quick fish to prepare that is light and a great partner to this white bean dish.

### ⊰ INGREDIENTS ⊱

- 1 onion
- 6 cloves
- 2 carrots

- ¾ pound dried white beans, soaked overnight in water to cover by 2 inches
- 3½ ounces Spanish chorizo

- ½ bunch fresh parsley
- 2 tablespoons balsamic vinegar
- 3 tablespoons unsalted butter

- Salt and freshly ground pepper
- 4 tilapia fillets
- 2 tablespoons extra-virgin olive oil

1. Gather your ingredients.

2. Peel the onion and insert the cloves. Peel the carrots.

3. In a large pot, combine the onion, carrots, beans, and fresh water to cover by 1 inch. Bring to a boil, and then reduce the heat and simmer for about 40 minutes or until the beans are tender but still a little firm.

4. Dice the chorizo. Remove the parsley leaves and chop.

5. Once the beans are cooked, remove the whole onion and carrots and drain any remaining water. Add the chorizo, balsamic vinegar, and 2 tablespoons of the butter.

6. Sprinkle the fish with salt and pepper. In a large skillet, heat the olive oil over high heat. Pan-sear the fillets for 2 to 3 minutes on each side. Melt the remaining 1 tablespoon of butter in the pan and drizzle over the fish. Sprinkle the parsley on the fish and beans.

### ⊰ KITCHEN NOTES ⊱
- Use another light white fish, like cod or sea bass.
- This white bean recipe is great with grilled or pan-seared pork chops.
- Drizzle a little red wine vinegar on your beans before serving.

# PAN-SEARED SALMON & LENTILS

SAUMON SAUTÉ AUX LENTILLES

*Serves 4*

Lentils and salmon have always been a wonderful combination. In this recipe we panfry the salmon
in olive oil and finish with brown butter, giving it a delicious nutty essence.

## ◄ INGREDIENTS ►

- 3 tablespoons unsalted butter
- 2 or 3 celery ribs, finely chopped
- 1 medium onion, finely chopped
- 1 medium carrot, finely chopped
- 1 tablespoon sherry vinegar
- ½ recipe Lentils (page 199)
- 1 teaspoon extra-virgin olive oil
- One 4½-ounce salmon fillet, skin on
- Salt and freshly ground pepper

1. Gather your ingredients.

2. Melt 1 tablespoon of the butter in a large pot and add the vegetables. Sweat for 5 to 7 minutes, depending on how finely your vegetables are cut, over medium heat, without browning. Add 1 tablespoon of the butter, the vinegar, and lentils. Stir and set aside.

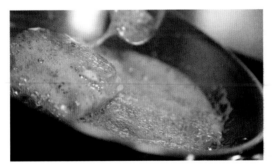

3. In a sauté pan over medium-high heat, heat the olive oil and sear the salmon fillet for about 2 minutes on each side. Melt the remaining 1 tablespoon of butter in the pan and drizzle over the fillet to finish. Season with salt and pepper.

# SALT-CRUSTED FISH
## BAR EN CROUTE DE SEL

*Serves 4*

This is a staple dish at our La Boulange Friday dinners. The aromas of the herbs and fish are intoxicating, and the combination of the fresh, crunchy vegetable salsa and the tender fish is outstanding. It is important to prepare and bake the fish right away. If you refrigerate the fish after it's been encrusted, it will fall apart. This is a wonderful weekend dish to prepare for friends and family when you have a little time to spend in the kitchen.

### ⊰ INGREDIENTS ⊱

*For the salt and Herbes de Provence dough and the fish*
- 4 cups all-purpose flour
- 5 cups gray sea salt (heavy grain)
- 8 egg whites

- 3½ cups Herbes de Provence
- 2 cups water
- One 3½-pound sea bass or red snapper, scales removed and gutted

- A few fennel fronds
- ½ bunch fresh cilantro
- ½ bunch fresh parsley
- 1 egg yolk, beaten

*For the mixed vegetable salsa*
- ¼ bunch cilantro
- ¼ bunch parsley
- ¼ bunch basil
- 1 shallot

- ½ onion
- 3 green onions
- 2 tomatoes
- ¼ fennel bulb
- ¼ yellow bell pepper
- ¼ red bell pepper

- ¼ green bell pepper
- 4 lemons
- 4 limes
- ½ cup extra-virgin olive oil

1. Gather your ingredients. Line a baking sheet with parchment paper. Preheat the oven to 425°F.

2. Mix the first four ingredients for the dough in a stand mixer, adding each ingredient gradually and increasing the speed as the dough becomes thicker and harder to mix. This is a dense dough, so you don't want to stress the mixer by adding the ingredients too quickly. Once all the dry ingredients are well combined, add the water, continuing to mix. If the dough is too sticky, add a little more flour.

3. Remove the dough and knead into a rectangular shape about 4 inches thick. Cut into two pieces, a third for the bottom and two-thirds for the top.

4. On a lightly floured surface, roll the smaller piece of dough, for the base, a little larger than the size of your fish. Transfer to the baking sheet.

5. Lay the fish on the dough and stuff with the fennel fronds, cilantro, and parsley. It is important to maintain the shape of the fish body, so make sure it is stuffed carefully. With kitchen scissors, cut the fin off the back of the fish. There should be about a 1-inch margin of exposed dough around the fish. Brush this area with a bit of water to help seal the top.

6. Roll out the second piece of dough on the work surface and lay it on top of the fish. Pinch the top and bottom crusts together to seal. With a knife, cut away the excess dough, leaving about ½ inch around the fish. Brush the entire surface with egg wash.

CONTINUEZ

*We know it's long, difficult, painful . . . but this one is so worth it!*

CONTINUEZ

7. Transfer the fish to a roasting pan and bake for 40 minutes. Meanwhile, make the salsa. Very finely chop all the herbs and vegetables and combine in a medium bowl.

8. Completely peel and segment 2 of the lemons and 3 of the limes. Remove the segments and squeeze the juice from the membranes with your hand. Juice the remaining 2 lemons and 1 lime and add the juice to your mix.

9. Add the lemon and lime segments to the bowl and then add the olive oil. Mix thoroughly.

10. To test the fish for doneness, pierce it in the center with a small sharp knife or metal skewer. Leave the object in the fish for 20 seconds, remove, and set under your lower lip. If it is hot, the fish is done. If not, let it cook for a few more minutes.

11. Cut around the base of the fish completely to remove the top crust. The steam will smell incredible.

12. Extract pieces of fish and divide among dinner plates. Spoon a generous amount of the salsa over the fish and serve.

# CHICKEN WITH OLIVES

## POULET AUX OLIVES

*Serves 4*

Quick and easy, this braised chicken is cooked in a white wine sauce with shallots. The green olives and thyme bring a classic Provençal touch.

### ⊰ INGREDIENTS ⊱

- 1 small shallot
- 11 ounces button mushrooms
- 3 tablespoons extra-virgin olive oil
- 1 whole chicken, quartered (legs and breasts, skin on)
- 2 tablespoons all-purpose flour
- ¾ cup white wine
- 4 cups chicken broth
- 2 sprigs fresh thyme
- 3 bay leaves
- ¾ cup green olives
- Salt and freshly ground black pepper

1. Gather your ingredients.

2. Peel and slice the shallot. Clean the mushrooms and cut into quarters.

3. In a large pot over medium heat, heat the olive oil and cook the shallots until translucent. Add the chicken and sear for 2 to 4 minutes on each side, until slightly browned. Sprinkle with the flour and cook for another 5 minutes on each side.

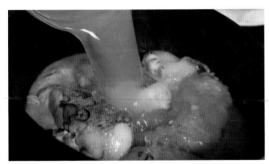

4. Add the white wine, reduce the heat to medium, and cook for 3 to 4 minutes. Add the chicken broth, thyme, and bay leaves, cover, and simmer for 40 minutes.

5. Remove the chicken and set aside. Add the mushrooms and olives to the broth and cook for 10 minutes.

6. Return the chicken to the pot. Remove the bay leaves, add salt and pepper to taste, and serve.

### ⊰ KITCHEN NOTES ⊱
- You can serve this in individual puff pastry shells.

# BOEUF BOURGUIGNON

*Serves 4*

An old-fashioned French dish, boeuf bourguignon is usually eaten in the winter. It's great to prepare on a Sunday and eat as leftovers during the week. Serve this with boiled potatoes, rice, or pasta. It even makes a delicious tartine, a favorite monthly special at La Boulange.

## ⊰ INGREDIENTS ⊱

- 4 carrots
- 1½ onions
- 4 green onions
- 3 tablespoons extra-virgin olive oil
- 2 pounds beef chuck cut into 2-inch chunks
- 1 tablespoon all-purpose flour
- 1½ bottles red wine
- 3 garlic cloves
- 3 sprigs fresh thyme
- 3 bay leaves
- Salt and freshly ground pepper

1. Gather your ingredients.

2. Peel the carrots and cut on a diagonal. Peel and thinly slice the onions. Prepare the green onions by removing the outer layer and cutting off the bottom and tip.

3. In a large pot over medium-high heat, heat the olive oil and add the beef. Sear the chunks until lightly browned.

4. Remove the beef from the pot and set aside. Reduce the heat to medium. Cook the onions until soft and translucent.

5. Return the beef to the pot.

6. Sprinkle the flour lightly over the beef. Stir well and cook for 3 minutes.

7. Add the wine, carrots, garlic cloves, thyme, and bay leaves. Bring to a boil. Reduce the heat so the wine is at a low simmer and cover. Simmer for about 2 hours and 50 minutes. The beef should be very tender.

8. Meanwhile, in a small saucepan, cook the green onions in boiling water for 4 to 5 minutes. They should be slightly crunchy. Plunge into an ice bath and set aside in the refrigerator.

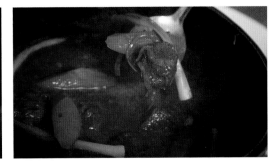

9. When the beef has finished cooking, add the green onions and cook for another 10 minutes. Remove the bay leaves. Add salt and pepper to taste, remove from the heat, and serve.

# LAMB SHANK CONFIT TARTINE
## TARTINE DE JARRET D'AGNEAU CONFIT

*Serves 2*

Alain, our chef de cuisine, loves lamb shank confit, especially when it's on a tartine. This is the type of tartine that you need to be patient with; otherwise you won't make it to the end (the lamb needs to cook for 4 to 5 hours).

### ⊰ INGREDIENTS ⊱

- 4 cups Lamb Jus (page 206) or beef broth
- 2 tablespoons canola oil
- 2 lamb shanks
- 3 bay leaves
- 2 sprigs fresh thyme
- 1 garlic bulb, halved
- Salt and freshly ground pepper
- 2 slices country bread, toasted

1. Gather your ingredients. If using the lamb jus, prepare it ahead of time.

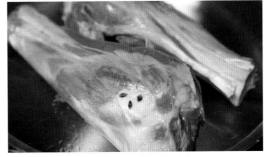

2. In a large sauté pan over medium-high heat, heat the canola oil and sear the lamb shanks on each side until lightly browned.

3. Transfer to a large saucepan and add the bay leaves, thyme, garlic, and lamb jus. Add enough water to cover the shanks. Bring the water to a boil, reduce the heat, and simmer, covered, for 4 hours. Continue to maintain the level of liquid by adding water for the first 3 hours. For the final hour let the liquid reduce. Season with salt and pepper.

4. Remove the lamb from the saucepan and set aside on a plate.

5. When cool enough to handle, remove the meat from the bone with your hands.

6. Shred the lamb into pieces and lay on the toasted bread.

### ⊰ KITCHEN NOTES ⊱
- It's great served with Farro Risotto (page 135) or with the American classic, mashed potatoes.

# CHICKEN TAGINE

### TAGINE DE POULET

❦

*Serves 4*

A *tagine* is a Moroccan meat, poultry, or vegetable stew flavored with fragrant spices. Dried or preserved fruit are common ingredients as well. *Tagine* also refers to the cooking vessel with a cone-shaped lid that traditionally is used to cook these stews.

#### ⤙ INGREDIENTS ⤚

- 3 small carrots
- 5 small waxy potatoes, such as Yukon gold
- 1 medium onion
- 1 tablespoon extra-virgin olive oil
- 1½ teaspoons ground cumin
- 1½ teaspoons ground cinnamon
- ¼ teaspoon cayenne pepper, or to taste
- 4 bone-in chicken legs
- 1 cup prunes
- Salt and freshly ground black pepper
- Fresh cilantro leaves for garnish

1. Gather your ingredients.

2. Peel the carrots and slice them on the diagonal ½ inch thick.

3. Peel the potatoes and slice them into ½-inch-thick rounds. Peel and thinly slice the onion.

4. In a large sauté pan over medium heat, heat the olive oil and add the spices. Cook, stirring, until fragrant and blended.

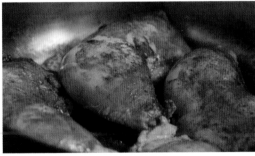

5. Add the chicken legs and cook on each side for about 2 minutes or until coated with spices and very lightly browned. Transfer the chicken to a plate and set aside.

6. Add the onions to the pan and sauté over medium heat for about 3 minutes, until they begin to soften.

7. Add the carrots and potatoes. Set the chicken legs on top of the vegetables in a single layer, and then scatter the prunes over the chicken. Season with salt and pepper.

8. Pour in just enough water to come almost all the way up the sides of the chicken, about ¾ cup. Bring to a boil over medium heat, and then reduce the heat to low to maintain a simmer.

9. Cover the pan and simmer until the chicken and vegetables are completely tender, about 1 hour. Serve garnished with the cilantro leaves.

# SUMMER COD SALAD

## SALADE DE POISSON BLANC AUX LÉGUMES CRUS

*Serves 2*

This is a great dish to make on the weekend, when you can enjoy the process.
The preparation of all of the vegetables takes time, but nothing is too difficult and it is well worth it.

### ⊰ INGREDIENTS ⊱

- 1 artichoke
- Juice of 1 lemon
- 4 asparagus stalks
- ½ shallot
- ½ fennel bulb
- 3 baby carrots
- 3 or 4 green onions

- 6 cherry tomatoes
- 1 celery rib
- 1 tablespoon extra-virgin olive oil
- Salt and freshly ground pepper

- 9 ounces cod fillet
- 4 tablespoons Lemon Vinaigrette (page 200)
- ¼ cup chopped fresh cilantro
- 1 tablespoon chopped fresh chervil

- 1 tablespoon chopped fresh parsley
- 3 tablespoons Jus de Crustacés (optional, page 205)

1. Gather your ingredients. Preheat the oven to 450°F.

2. Prepare the artichoke. Remove the outer leaves and using a paring knife, clean the base. Remove the top three-quarters, so you are left with just the base.

3. With your knife, cut away everything but the core. Cut the core into small wedges, making sure to remove the hair. Place the wedges in a bowl with the lemon juice to avoid oxidation.

4. Peel and thinly slice the asparagus, shallot, fennel, and carrots. Thinly slice the green onions. Quarter the cherry tomatoes and cut the celery into ½-inch pieces. Combine all the vegetables in a bowl.

5. Drizzle the olive oil on a baking sheet and sprinkle with salt and pepper. Cut the cod fillet into about 2½- to 3-inch pieces and drizzle with 2 tablespoons of the lemon vinaigrette. Bake for 7 to 10 minutes.

6. Toss all the vegetables with the remaining lemon vinaigrette and add the cilantro, chervil, and parsley. Spoon the *jus de crustacés* over the fish, if desired.

### ⊰ KITCHEN NOTES ⊱

- You can use frozen or canned artichoke hearts instead of fresh.

# SAUTÉED ASPARAGUS WITH PARMESAN

## ASPERGES RÔTIES AU PARMESAN

*Serves 4*

This is a wonderful, simple side dish. It's a great preparation of asparagus, and a perfect way to add some green to your meal. Take care not to overcook the asparagus; it's best when there's just a hint of crunch.

### ◄ INGREDIENTS ►

- 1 bunch asparagus
- 1 tablespoon extra-virgin olive oil

- ¼ cup grated Parmesan cheese
- 2 tablespoons balsamic vinegar

- 1 tablespoon unsalted butter
- Arugula for garnish

- 4 Parmesan Crisps (page 198)

1. Gather your ingredients.

2. In a pot of salted boiling water, cook the asparagus for 2 to 3 minutes. Drain and plunge into an ice water bath. Drain again.

3. In a medium skillet over medium heat, heat the olive oil and sauté the asparagus just until coated with the oil.

4. Sprinkle with the Parmesan cheese.

5. Remove the asparagus and transfer to a serving plate. Add the balsamic vinegar and butter to the skillet. Deglaze for a few seconds, scraping up any browned bits from the pan.

6. Drizzle the balsamic glaze over the asparagus and top with the arugula and Parmesan crisps.

### ◄ KITCHEN NOTES ►

- We like to finish with a little butter, but you can do without if you prefer.

*Main Dishes, Monthly Specials & La Boulange Fridays*

# SWEETS & DESSERTS

# TROPÉZIENNE

*Serves 4*

This cute little pastry hails from Saint Tropez and was a favorite of Brigitte Bardot's. It's quite an original and distinctive little dessert—soft, light, and very easy to make. Use the best brioche buns you can find.

## ⊰ INGREDIENTS ⊱

- ¾ cup heavy cream
- ¼ cup honey
- 1¼ cups Pastry Cream (page 194)
- 4 brioche buns, halved
- Confectioners' sugar for dusting

1. Gather your ingredients.

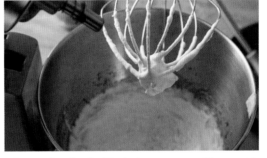

2. In a medium bowl, whip the heavy cream and honey with an electric mixer until soft peaks form.

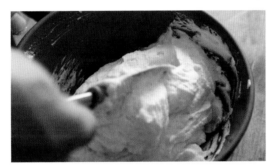

3. Put the pastry cream in a large bowl, and fold in the cream and honey. Mix slowly, being careful not to stir too much. Spoon the mix onto the brioche bases, and cover with the tops. Sprinkle with confectioners' sugar.

## ⊰ KITCHEN NOTES ⊱
- Use cocoa powder in the pastry cream filling, or add berries for a splash of color.

# RUSTIC APPLE TART
## TARTE AUX POMMES

❧❦❧

*Serves 8*

This recipe is just like the one my mother used to make. The tart apples,
combined with a little sugar and a great applesauce, are a perfect combination.

### ❧ INGREDIENTS ❧

- Savory Shortcrust Dough (page 192) or store-bought
- 4 Granny Smith apples
- 4 tablespoons granulated sugar
- ¾ cup applesauce

1. Gather your ingredients. Have an 11-inch tart pan with a removable bottom ready. Preheat the oven to 400°F.

2. Roll out the dough and press it into the tart pan. Trim off the excess dough from the edges.

3. Peel and core the apples and cut into 1-inch cubes. Transfer to a bowl and mix with 3 tablespoons of the sugar.

4. Spread out on a baking sheet and roast for 20 minutes.

5. Combine the roasted apple chunks with the applesauce in a bowl.

6. Pour the apple mixture into the tart shell. Sprinkle with the remaining 1 tablespoon of sugar. Bake for 35 to 40 minutes. Let cool for about 20 minutes before serving.

# LE DÔME

*Makes 12 to 15 domes*

Chocolate and vanilla crème sandwiched between two almond meringues, covered in crème and chocolate shavings. A perfect indulgence.

## ◃ INGREDIENTS ▹

*For the meringue*
- 4 egg whites
- 1 cup sugar
- ½ cup hazelnut meal

- Two 3-ounce bars white chocolate for shaving
- Two 3-ounce bars dark chocolate for shaving

*For the chantilly*
- 1 cup heavy cream
- 1 tablespoon sugar

*For the vanilla crème*
- ½ cup Pastry Cream (page 194)
- 2 teaspoons vanilla extract

*For the chocolate crème*
- ½ cup Pastry Cream (page 194)

- Seeds from ½ a vanilla bean
- ½ cup bittersweet chocolate pieces for melting

1. Gather your ingredients. Preheat the oven to 200°F.

2. To make the meringue, whip the egg whites on high speed with ⅓ cup of the sugar until soft peaks form. Add another ⅓ cup of the sugar and whip until stiff peaks form. Beat in the remaining ⅓ cup of sugar. Fold in the hazelnut meal.

3. Using a pastry bag (or a plastic storage bag with the corner cut off), pipe twelve to fifteen flat meringues on one baking sheet.

4. On a second baking sheet, pipe twelve to fifteen domed meringues. Bake for 1 hour and 30 minutes. Tap a meringue to see if it's dry and remove immediately.

5. While the meringues are baking, with a peeler, shave ¾ cup each from the white and dark chocolate bars and refrigerate.

6. To make the chantilly (whipped cream), combine the heavy cream and sugar in a medium bowl and beat with an electric mixer until stiff peaks form.

7. To make the vanilla crème, put the pastry cream in a large bowl and add the vanilla extract. Scrape the vanilla seeds into the bowl and fold in half of the chantilly. For the chocolate crème, melt the chocolate over very low heat.

8. Put the pastry cream in a large bowl and fold in the melted chocolate until combined. Fold in the remaining chantilly. Spread the vanilla crème over half the meringue bottoms and top with domed meringues. Spread a layer of the crème over the domed tops.

9. Repeat the process with the chocolate crème and remaining meringues. Pour the dark and white chocolate shavings over the meringues. Serve right away or store in the refrigerator.

# CANNELÉS WITH CARAMELIZED BANANAS

## CANNELÉS AUX BANANES CARAMÉLISÉES

❖

*Serves 4*

*Cannelés* hail from Bordeaux. There, they are always served warm out of the oven, all by themselves. This recipe shows you a great way to turn *cannelés* into a delicious dessert for all seasons. Start with *cannelés* purchased from a French bakery (preferably ours!).

### ◄ INGREDIENTS ►

- 2 bananas (not fully ripe)
- 2 tablespoons unsalted butter
- 2 tablespoons sugar
- Crème Anglaise (page 193)
- 4 cannelés, halved

1. Gather your ingredients.

2. Peel and cut each banana on a diagonal. Melt the butter in a large skillet over medium heat. Add the sugar and mix well.

3. Add the bananas and cook on both sides until nicely browned, 4 to 5 minutes total. Set aside. Spoon crème anglaise onto each plate and top with two *cannelé* halves and two banana pieces.

### ◄ KITCHEN NOTES ►

- If you can't find *cannelés*, Fondant au Chocolat (page 171) is also delicious with this recipe.
- After removing the bananas from the heat, add a splash of rum to the pan and then stir to coat the bananas.
- Serve the *cannelés* and bananas with vanilla or caramel ice cream instead of crème anglaise.

# FLOATING ISLANDS
## ÎLES FLOTTANTES

*Serves 4*

This is a simplified version of a French classic and is one of my kids' favorite desserts. The meringue "islands" are light and airy, and the crème anglaise that they float on is rich and creamy. The toasted almond garnish adds the perfect amount of crunchiness. Have the crème anglaise and caramel already made for a fun last-minute dessert after a dinner with friends.

### ◄ INGREDIENTS ►

- ¼ cup sliced almonds
- 8 egg whites
- Pinch of salt
- ¼ cup sugar

- Crème Anglaise (page 193)
- Caramel Sauce (page 192) or store-bought (preferably from us!)

1. Gather your ingredients.

2. In a large skillet over medium heat, toast the almonds until browned and fragrant, 2 to 3 minutes. Transfer to a bowl and let cool.

3. In a large bowl, beat the egg whites and salt with an electric mixer on high speed until soft peaks form.

4. Add the sugar and beat for about 1 minute more.

5. Line a large plate with parchment paper. Spoon four generous mounds of the beaten egg whites onto the plate. Microwave, uncovered, for 30 to 45 seconds on high power.

6. Pour enough crème anglaise into a bowl to float an island in the crème, and drizzle with caramel. Sprinkle with toasted almonds.

### ◄ KITCHEN NOTES ►

- For a lemony twist, add grated lemon zest to the egg whites.
- Serve with caramelized pineapple or banana on the side.

# FONDANT AU CHOCOLAT

*Serves 10*

This chocolate dessert is deceptively simple. Once you try it, you'll be making it every weekend and for every occasion. Baked just right, the center will ooze molten chocolate. (*Fondant* means "melting.")

## ‹ INGREDIENTS ›

- ¾ cup light brown sugar
- 1 tablespoon plus
  1 teaspoon all-purpose
  flour
- 3 eggs

- ½ cup (1 stick) plus
  1 tablespoon unsalted
  butter
- 6 ounces dark chocolate

1. Gather your ingredients. Butter a 12-cup muffin pan. Preheat the oven to 350°F.

2. In a large bowl, mix the brown sugar, flour, and eggs until well combined.

3. In a small saucepan on low heat, melt the butter and chocolate together, being careful not to burn the chocolate. Remove from the heat, pour into the egg mixture, and stir well. Divide evenly among the cups in the muffin pan. Bake for 10 to 12 minutes, until the middle of each fondant has crusted over. Let cool in the pan.

## ‹ KITCHEN NOTES ›

- For a brownie consistency, bake for a few minutes longer.
- Use 6-ounce ramekins instead of a muffin pan for individual servings right out of the oven.
- Great with ice cream and berries, candied nuts, melted caramel, or peanut butter.

# KINGS CAKE
## GALETTE DES ROIS

❖

*Serves 6 to 8*

Dating back to the Middle Ages, this traditional cake from France contains a lucky charm (*une fève*). Whoever finds it in his or her slice of cake becomes king or queen for the day. We created a series of special charms just for our *galettes des rois*, each an icon of San Francisco. For the month of January, we give away one charm with every galette we sell.

◄ INGREDIENTS ►

- 2 frozen puff pastry sheets, defrosted in the refrigerator
- ½ cup (1 stick) plus 1 tablespoon unsalted butter
- ½ cup plus 2 tablespoons sugar
- 3 eggs
- 2 teaspoons all-purpose flour
- 1 teaspoon salt
- 1 cup plus 2 tablespoons almond meal
- ½ cup Pastry Cream (page 194)
- 1½ tablespoons dark rum

1. Gather your ingredients. Preheat the oven to 375°F. Cut each puff pastry sheet into a circle about 11 inches in diameter and store in the freezer until ready to use.

2. In the bowl of a stand mixer on low to medium speed, beat the butter and sugar until light and creamy. Beat in 2 of the eggs, the flour, salt, and almond meal, one at a time.

3. Add the pastry cream and rum and mix at medium speed until blended.

4. Lay one puff pastry round on a baking sheet. Spread out the filling, leaving 1 inch of exposed dough around the edge.

5. Beat the remaining egg, brush the edge with the egg wash, and cover with the second round of puff pastry. Press the edges with your fingertips to seal; make sure to do this thoroughly so almond cream doesn't seep out while it bakes.

6. Brush the top with the egg wash and make four small slits with the tip of a knife. Bake for 40 minutes or until golden brown. Cool 45 minutes to 1 hour before serving.

# RED FRUIT GRATIN

### GRATIN DE FRUITS ROUGES

*Serves 1*

This is a super-simple dessert, perfect for a hot summer night.

## ◂ INGREDIENTS ▸

- 2 tablespoons honey
- 3 egg yolks
- 1 tablespoon water
- 2 strawberries, halved
- 10 raspberries
- 6 blackberries
- 15 blueberries
- 2 tablespoons Red Fruit Coulis (page 198)

1. Gather your ingredients. Preheat the broiler.

2. In the bowl of a stand mixer, combine the honey, egg yolks, and water. Mix on high speed until thick and four times greater in volume. Toss the fruit together in a bowl.

3. Pour the red fruit coulis onto an ovenproof plate, add the mixed fruit, and top with the egg mixture. Broil for 2 to 3 minutes or until golden brown. Serve warm.

## ◂ KITCHEN NOTES ▸

- The gratin is terrific with vanilla ice cream
- Use your favorite mix of berries.

# MINI FLAN TARTS

### MINI FLAN

*Serves 2*

A flan tart is a classic dessert. It is simple and traditional, and wonderful just a little warm. Enjoyed by kids of all ages.

### ◄ INGREDIENTS ►

- 1 frozen puff pastry sheet, thawed in the refrigerator
- 1¼ cups Pastry Cream (page 194)

1. Gather your ingredients. Have two individual tart pans ready. Preheat the oven to 400°F.

2. Use the bottom of a tart pan to trace two circles in the puff pastry the size of the tart pans. Press the dough into the pans and score the bottoms.

3. Divide the pastry cream evenly between the tart shells. Bake for 30 to 35 minutes, or until the tops are golden brown. Cool for 15 minutes, remove the tarts from the pans, and cool for another 15 minutes.

# ICE CREAM CAKE SURPRISE
## VACHERIN SURPRISE

*Serves 8 to 10*

Impress all of your friends with this original and delicious cake. Make sure to use a mix of colors and flavors, to really make every bite a surprise. We recommend using a few sorbets and a few ice creams.

### ⊰ INGREDIENTS ⊱

- Unbaked batter of Macarons de San Francisco (page 185)
- 3 pints ice cream, any flavor except vanilla
- 3 pints sorbet, any flavor
- ½ gallon vanilla ice cream
- Whipped cream for garnish (optional)
- Confectioners' sugar for sprinkling (optional)
- Fresh fruit for garnish (optional)

1. Gather your ingredients. Have a 9-inch aluminum baking ring ready. Preheat the oven to 375°F.

2. Make the Macarons de San Francisco batter. On a parchment-lined baking sheet, pipe the batter into two 9-inch spiral cookies. Bake for 22 to 25 minutes or until golden brown.

3. Remove from the oven and let cool. Once cooled, use the baking ring to shape an even, exact circle cookie. Leave the ring in place.

4. Place two scoops of each flavor on top of one cookie.

5. In a stand mixer, mix the vanilla ice cream to soften.

6. Spread the softened vanilla ice cream over the ice cream and sorbet scoops, filling the baking ring.

7. Top with the second spiral cookie. Place the entire baking sheet in the freezer for 1 hour.

8. Remove from the freezer and take off the baking molds just before serving. Decorate with whipped cream, confectioners' sugar, and/or fresh fruit.

# CHOCOLATE CHIP SHORTBREAD COOKIES

## SABLÉS AUX PETITS CHOCOLATS

*Makes 30 cookies*

This is La Boulange's twist on the classic chocolate chip cookie. We make it with shortbread dough.
Make the dough ahead of time, freeze it, and pop it in the oven just before you want to serve.

### ‹ INGREDIENTS ›

- 1¼ cups (2½ sticks) unsalted butter, at room temperature
- ½ cup sugar
- 3 cups all-purpose flour
- ½ teaspoon sea salt
- 1 teaspoon vanilla extract
- 1 tablespoon water
- 1 cup mini chocolate chips
- 1 egg for egg wash

1. Gather your ingredients.

2. Cut the butter into cubes. In a large bowl, mix the sugar and butter with a wooden spoon until well combined.

3. Add the flour and salt and use your hands to mix until you have a dough with a crumbly consistency. Add the vanilla extract and water, and mix again with your hands.

4. Add the chocolate chips and mix.

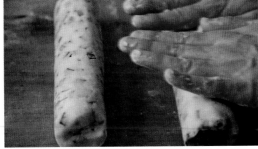

5. Roll the dough into one large log. Cut in half lengthwise, and roll each piece to create two equal logs, about 2 inches in diameter. Wrap in plastic and refrigerate for 2 hours.

6. Preheat the oven to 350°F. Cut the dough into rounds ⅓ inch thick. Arrange as many as you can fit on a nonstick baking sheet or parchment paper-lined sheet. Brush with the egg wash, if desired. Bake for 15 to 18 minutes, until golden brown. Repeat with the remaining dough.

# PARMESAN & CAYENNE SHORTBREAD COOKIES

## SABLÉS AU PARMESAN ET CAYENNE

*Makes 18 cookies*

These spicy little buttery cookies are perfect for an appetizer or a snack on their own. They're quite addictive, so be careful!

### ⊰ INGREDIENTS ⊱

- 1 cup (2 sticks) plus 1 tablespoon unsalted butter
- 2 cups all-purpose flour
- ½ teaspoon salt
- 2½ cups grated Parmesan cheese (about ½ pound)
- ½ teaspoon cayenne pepper
- 1 egg for egg wash

1. Gather your ingredients.

2. Cut the butter into cubes. In a large bowl, mix the butter, flour, and salt with your hands until you have a dough with a crumbly consistency.

3. Add the Parmesan cheese and mix again. Add the cayenne and mix again. If the dough is too dry, add 1 to 2 teaspoons of water.

4. Knead the dough on a work surface to thoroughly blend and roll into a square log about 12 inches long. Wrap in plastic and refrigerate for a minimum of 1 hour.

5. Preheat the oven to 350°F. Cut the dough into pieces ⅓ inch thick.

6. Arrange as many as you can fit on a nonstick baking sheet or parchment paper-lined sheet. Brush with the egg wash, and bake for 15 to 18 minutes until golden brown. Repeat with the remaining dough.

### ⊰ KITCHEN NOTES ⊱

- Substitute cheese and cayenne with thyme and cracked pepper for an herbed shortbread cookie.

*Sweets & Desserts*

# MACARONS DE SAN FRANCISCO

*Makes 30 macarons*

As a little boy I remember going to Saint-Emilion with my parents to buy cases of wine. Every time, we stopped at this really tiny pastry shop and bought the delicious *macarons de Saint-Emilion.* I adored them. Today, we bake our own version of this macaron using native California almonds, mixed with hazelnut, egg white, and sugar. That's it—*c'est tout!*

## ⤝ INGREDIENTS ⤞

- 3¾ cups hazelnut meal
- 2 cups plus 1 tablespoon almond meal
- 1¾ cups sugar
- 9 egg whites

1. Gather your ingredients. Preheat the oven to 375°F.

2. Mix the hazelnut meal, almond meal, and 1¼ cups of the sugar in a medium bowl.

3. In a large bowl, beat the egg whites with an electric mixer until soft peaks begin to form. Add 2½ tablespoons of the remaining sugar.

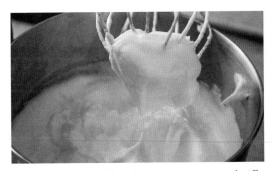

4. Continue to beat, adding the remaining sugar, until stiff peaks form.

5. Slowly fold the dry mixture into the egg whites until combined.

6. Using a tablespoon, dollop the dough onto a baking sheet lined with parchment paper and bake for 16 to 18 minutes until lightly golden on the edges.

## ⤝ KITCHEN NOTES ⤞

- These classic little cookies will complement coffee, tea, hot chocolate, Champagne (trust us), or white or red wine.
- You can add chocolate chips or coconut shavings (although *macarons de Saint-Emilion* traditionalists will turn in their graves).
- Make a little sandwich with your favorite jam in between two cookies.

# LUNETTES

❖◆❖

*Makes 8 to 10 lunettes*

Lunettes bring me back to my childhood in France, where they were a favorite afterschool treat.
These cookies are called *lunettes*, which means "reading glasses" in French, because of the two jam circles.

## ◄ INGREDIENTS ►

- ½ cup (1 stick) plus 6 tablespoons unsalted butter
- 2 cups all-purpose flour
- 1 cup sugar
- 1 cup hazelnut meal
- 3 eggs
- 1 teaspoon vanilla extract
- Powdered sugar for dusting
- About ½ cup fruit jam total, in 2 flavors (¼ cup of each, preferably from La Boulange!)

1. Gather your ingredients. Have ready a ribbed 3-inch-square cookie cutter (or any cutter will work) and a ribbed 1-inch-round cookie cutter.

2. Cut the butter into cubes. In a large bowl, combine the butter, flour, sugar, and hazelnut meal. Mix with your hands until you have a dough with a crumbly consistency.

3. Add 2 of the eggs and the vanilla and mix well with your hands.

4. Knead the dough on a work surface and form into a large ball. Dust with flour and wrap in plastic. Refrigerate for at least 2 hours and up to 24.

5. Preheat the oven to 350°F. With a floured rolling pin, roll out the dough until about ½ inch thick.

6. Using the square cookie cutter, cut as many cookies as possible from your dough.

7. Lay the squares on a baking sheet lined with parchment paper. Using the round cutter, cut two holes in each of half of the squares. Those will be the top cookies.

8. Beat the third egg in a dish and brush all the squares with the egg wash. Bake for 15 minutes or until light golden brown.

9. Sprinkle the lunette tops with powdered sugar. Spoon ½ tablespoon of each jam flavor in the middle of each bottom cookie (the ones with no holes). Cover with the tops.

# LES CROQUETS DE BORDEAUX

*Makes 40 croquets*

These cookies are a specialty of the Medoc region of Bordeaux. Wonderful with wine and, of course, coffee, these crunchy treats are perfect for dipping. If we had to make a comparison, we'd say they're the French cousin of Italian biscotti.

## ◄ INGREDIENTS ►

- 1⅓ cups whole almonds
- 1¾ cups sugar
- ¾ cup plus 2 teaspoons all-purpose flour
- 3 cups almond meal
- 1 tablespoon baking powder
- ½ teaspoon salt
- ½ cup (1 stick) plus 2 tablespoons unsalted butter
- 3 eggs
- Zest of 1 lemon

1. Gather your ingredients. Preheat the oven to 350°F.

2. Roast the almonds on a baking sheet for 10 to 12 minutes. Cool and chop.

3. In a large bowl, combine the sugar, flour, almond meal, baking powder, salt, and butter. Mix with your hands until you have a dough with a crumbly consistency.

4. Add 2 of the eggs and the lemon zest, and mix again.

5. Add the almond pieces and mix.

6. Knead the dough on a work surface and then roll into a 12-inch-long log with your hands.

7. Press to flatten into a quarter of a baking sheet. Freeze uncovered for a minimum of 1 hour.

8. Remove the dough from the freezer and cut in half lengthwise, then cut into ½-inch-thick slices.

9. Place the cookies on a baking sheet covered with parchment paper. Beat the remaining egg and brush the cookies with the egg wash. Bake for 12 to 15 minutes or until golden brown.

# BASES, DRESSINGS & SAUCES

# SAVORY SHORTCRUST DOUGH

## PATE BRISÉE

*Makes enough for one 11-inch tart shell*

### ⊰ INGREDIENTS ⊱

- 2½ cups all-purpose flour
- 10 tablespoons (1¼ sticks) cold unsalted butter, cut into cubes
- ¾ teaspoon salt
- 1 egg, lightly beaten
- ¼ cup cold water
- ½ teaspoon fresh lemon juice

1. Gather your ingredients.

2. Put the flour in a medium bowl. Mix the butter into the flour until you have small chunks.

3. Add the salt, and with your hands, mix the butter, flour, and salt until roughly combined. Add the egg, water, and lemon juice. Mix again with your hands until well combined. Shape into a ball, wrap in plastic, and store in the refrigerator for 1 hour before using, or up to 2 days.

# CARAMEL SAUCE

## SAUCE CARAMEL

*Makes about 1 cup*

### ⊰ INGREDIENTS ⊱

- ⅓ cup heavy cream
- ½ vanilla bean
- ½ tablespoon unsalted butter
- 1 teaspoon salt
- ½ cup granulated sugar

1. In a small saucepan over medium-high heat, bring the cream, vanilla bean, butter, and salt to a boil. Reduce the heat to low and keep warm while you caramelize the sugar. In a large saucepan, heat the sugar over low heat. Cook, stirring, until the sugar is completely dissolved and turns golden brown.

2. Add the cream mixture to the sugar, a little at a time, stirring constantly.

3. Remove from the heat and continue to stir until you have a smooth, creamy sauce. It will keep, covered, in the refrigerator for up to 1 week.

# CRÈME ANGLAISE

*Makes 1 cup*

A crème anglaise in just a few minutes? Are you kidding? This recipe is a quick-and-easy take on the traditional preparation. It's perfect when you're pressed for time. There are many ways to vary the flavor (see Kitchen Notes). Simply put, this is a convenient *and* delicious recipe.

## ◄ INGREDIENTS ►

- ½ cup milk
- ½ cup heavy cream
- 2½ tablespoons sugar
- 2 egg yolks
- ½ teaspoon vanilla extract

1. Gather your ingredients.

2. Combine the milk and cream in a microwave-safe bowl. Whisk to blend, and heat for 2 minutes at high power in the microwave.

3. Add the sugar to the hot milk and cream mixture. Add the egg yolks and vanilla and whisk well.

4. Microwave for 1 minute longer, whisk again, and serve. You can store the crème anglaise, covered, in the refrigerator for up to 3 days or in the freezer for up to 2 months.

## ◄ KITCHEN NOTES ►

- Replace the vanilla with rum, lemon zest, cocoa powder, coconut extract, or even pistachio paste for a different flavor.

# PASTRY CREAM

*Makes just over 4 cups*

## ⊰ INGREDIENTS ⊱

- 2 cups milk
- 2 tablespoons vanilla extract
- ⅓ cup plus 2 tablespoons sugar
- 6 egg yolks
- 3½ tablespoons all-purpose flour

1. Gather your ingredients.

2. In a medium saucepan on low heat, warm the milk. Add the vanilla and half of the sugar, whisking gently constantly. Maintain at a simmer.

3. In a large bowl, combine the egg yolks and the rest of the sugar and mix well.

4. Add flour in three parts, whisking well after each addition.

5. Add about ⅓ cup of the hot milk to the egg mixture and whisk. Transfer the egg mixture back to the saucepan and raise the heat to medium.

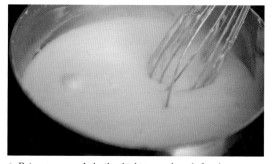

6. Bring to a gentle boil, whisking, and cook for about 2 minutes.

7. Remove from the heat. Use right away or let cool and store, covered, in the refrigerator for up to 3 days.

# CARAMELIZED ONIONS

OIGNONS CARAMÉLISÉS

*Makes 1 cup*

Caramelized onions are easy to make and great to have on hand. They can be used to add an extra layer of delicious flavor in many different ways—as a pizza topping, a burger topping, a garnish on a steak, a twist on your favorite salad, or baked into macaroni and cheese, just to name a few. We have two ways that we like to make them: one way, the main recipe way, includes balsamic vinegar and has fewer onions and a shorter cooking time. The variation has no balsamic vinegar, uses more onions, and has a longer cooking time.

## ⊰ INGREDIENTS ⊱

- 2 red onions
- 3 tablespoons unsalted butter
- 1 tablespoon sugar
- 3 tablespoons balsamic vinegar
- Salt and freshly ground pepper

1. Gather your ingredients.

2. Peel and thinly slice the onions.

3. Melt the butter in a large sauté pan or skillet over medium heat. Add the sugar.

4. Add the onions and stir to coat with the butter. Cook, stirring occasionally. After about 20 minutes, the onions should be softened and slightly caramelized. Add the balsamic vinegar and salt and pepper to taste.

5. Continue to cook, stirring frequently, until the onions are meltingly tender and deeply caramelized, about 5 to 10 more minutes.

6. Use the onions right away or cool and store in the refrigerator in an airtight container. The onions will keep for up to 5 days.

## ⊰ VARIATION ⊱

*Slow-Cooked Caramelized Onions*

1. Use 3 white onions instead of 2 red.

2. Use the same amount of butter and sugar, but omit the balsamic vinegar.

3. Cook the onions for a total of 45 minutes to 1 hour, until they are meltingly tender and deeply caramelized.

## ⊰ KITCHEN NOTES ⊱

- When the onions are done, add chopped fresh herbs, such as thyme, rosemary, or oregano, depending on the flavors in the dish to which you'll be adding the onions.

*Bases, Dressings & Sauces*

# CROUTONS

*Makes about 2½ cups*

Simple, buttery croutons are a must-have for adding wonderful texture to salads and soups of all kinds.
Brioche, sandwich bread, and focaccia work best for making light, crisp croutons, which are perfect for garnishing dishes
with delicate textures and flavors. It's best to use bread that's one or two days old.

## ⤙ INGREDIENTS ⤚

- 2 pounds brioche, *pain de mie*, or focaccia
- 3 tablespoons unsalted butter

1. Gather your ingredients.

2. Cut the bread into ½-inch cubes. You should have about 3 cups.

3. Melt the butter in a large skillet or sauté pan over medium heat. Add the bread cubes and cook, stirring frequently, until crisp and golden brown, about 5 to 7 minutes. Use right away or store at room temperature for up to 3 days.

## ⤙ KITCHEN NOTES ⤚

- Toss chopped fresh herbs, such as thyme and rosemary, into the croutons after toasting.
- Add crushed garlic to the melted butter for garlic croutons.

# PERSILLADE

*Makes about ⅓ to ½ cup*

## ⤙ INGREDIENTS ⤚

- ¼ cup plus 1 tablespoon parsley leaves
- 5 garlic cloves

1. Gather your ingredients.

2. Finely chop the parsley and garlic separately.

3. Combine and finely chop again, making sure the consistency is uniform. Transfer to a bowl.

# EGGPLANT CAVIAR

## CAVIAR D'AUBERGINE

*Serves 4*

### ◄ INGREDIENTS ►

- 2 eggplants
- 6 garlic cloves, 3 quartered

- 3 tablespoons extra-virgin olive oil, plus extra for drizzling

- 1 shallot
- 6 to 7 fresh basil leaves
- ¼ cup grated Parmesan cheese

- Salt and freshly ground pepper

1. Gather your ingredients. Preheat the oven to 400°F.

2. Lay the eggplants on a large sheet of aluminum foil. Make about six slits in each eggplant with the tip of a knife, and insert the garlic clove quarters in the slits.

3. Drizzle the eggplants with olive oil, and fold over the edges of the aluminum foil to make a pouch. Close the pouch and roast the eggplants for about 1 hour and 20 minutes, or until the meat is very soft.

4. Finely chop the shallot and remaining garlic. Thinly slice the basil.

5. Remove the eggplants from the oven and cut in half lengthwise. Remove meat with a spoon and chop well. Set aside in a bowl.

6. In a sauté pan over medium-high heat, heat the 3 tablespoons of olive oil and sweat the garlic and shallots for 1 to 2 minutes. Reduce the heat to medium and add the eggplant. Cook, stirring, for 5 minutes. Add the Parmesan cheese, basil, and salt and pepper to taste. Use right away or cool and store in the refrigerator for up to 3 days.

### ◄ KITCHEN NOTES ►
- The eggplant caviar can be eaten hot or cold. Either way, it's delicious on a tartine.

# RED FRUIT COULIS

COULIS DE FRUITS ROUGES

*Makes 2 cups*

### ‹ INGREDIENTS ›

- 1 cup water
- ½ cup sugar
- Juice of ½ lemon
- ½ pound raspberries

1. Gather your ingredients.

2. In a medium saucepan, combine the water, sugar, and lemon juice and bring to a boil. Cook, stirring, until the sugar is dissolved. Remove from the heat and cool.

3. Transfer the berries and cooled syrup to a blender, and blend for 2 to 3 minutes. Push through a strainer set over a bowl to remove the seeds. Best eaten right away, but you can store in the refrigerator for 2 to 3 days.

### ‹ KITCHEN NOTES ›

- Use the coulis to make a sorbet. It's also delicious over whipped cream, French toast or pancakes, ice cream, or chocolate fondant.

# PARMESAN CRISP

DENTELLE DE PARMESAN

*Makes 1 crisp*

### ‹ INGREDIENTS ›

- ¼ cup plus 2 tablespoons freshly shredded Parmesan

1. Heat a sauté pan over medium-high heat and sprinkle the Parmesan cheese in a circle.

2. Let it cook until browned, about 4 minutes.

3. Peel off the crisp with a spatula and set on a plate to cool.

*La Boulange Café Cooking at Home*

# LENTILS
LENTILLES

*Serves 4 to 6*

## ⊰ INGREDIENTS ⊱

- 5 whole cloves
- ½ white onion

- One 1-pound bag lentils
- 1 carrot

- 4 bay leaves
- 1 small bunch thyme

- Salt and freshly ground pepper

1. Gather your ingredients.

2. Insert the cloves in the onion. In a large pot, combine the onion, lentils, carrot, bay leaves, and thyme.

3. Add enough water to equal three times the volume of the lentils. Bring to a boil and cook for about 30 minutes or until tender. Drain the remaining liquid. Remove the onion, carrot, bay leaves, and thyme. Season the lentils with salt and pepper. Store, covered, in the refrigerator for up to 1 week.

# BALSAMIC VINAIGRETTE
VINAIGRETTE AU BALSAMIQUE

*Makes about ¼ cup*

## ⊰ INGREDIENTS ⊱

- 2 tablespoons balsamic vinegar

- 2 pinches of salt

- Pinch of freshly ground pepper

- 2 tablespoons extra-virgin olive oil

1. Gather your ingredients.

2. Always start with vinegar. Pour it into a small bowl, dissolve the salt in it, and add the pepper.

3. Whisk in the olive oil, continue to whisk until the vinaigrette emulsifies. Store, covered, in the refrigerator for up to 1 month.

## ⊰ KITCHEN NOTES ⊱
- For a more acidic vinaigrette, use half red wine vinegar and half balsamic.
- We love to use Dijon mustard in this vinaigrette. Add 1 tablespoon just before adding the oil.

# LEMON VINAIGRETTE

## VINAIGRETTE AU CITRON

❦

*Makes about ¼ cup*

◃ INGREDIENTS ▹

- Juice of 1 lemon
- 2 pinches of salt
- Pinch of freshly ground pepper
- 1 teaspoon Dijon mustard
- 3 tablespoons extra-virgin olive oil

1. Gather your ingredients.

2. Pour the lemon juice into a small bowl, dissolve the salt in it, and add the pepper. Whisk in the Dijon.

3. Finish by whisking in the olive oil and continuing to whisk until the vinaigrette emulsifies.

# CAESAR DRESSING

## SAUCE CÉSAR

❦

*Makes ½ cup*

◃ INGREDIENTS ▹

- 3 garlic cloves
- 1 egg yolk
- 1 teaspoon mustard
- Juice of 1 lemon
- 1 tablespoon shredded Parmesan cheese
- 1 tablespoon extra-virgin olive oil
- 1 teaspoon heavy cream

1. Gather your ingredients.

2. Mince the garlic. In a small bowl, whisk together the garlic, egg yolk, mustard, lemon juice, and Parmesan cheese. Slowly whisk in the olive oil.

3. While still whisking, slowly add the cream. Store, covered, in the refrigerator for up to 2 days.

◃ KITCHEN NOTES ▹

- You can thicken the dressing with anchovy paste or crushed anchovies.

La Boulange Café Cooking at Home

# MAYONNAISE

*Makes about ½ cup*

## ⊰ INGREDIENTS ⊱

- 1 egg yolk
- Pinch of salt
- 1 teaspoon Dijon mustard
- 1 teaspoon fresh lemon juice
- ½ cup vegetable oil or extra-virgin olive oil

1. Gather your ingredients.

2. Whisk the egg yolk, salt, and mustard well in a small bowl. Add the lemon juice. Very slowly, whisk in the oil, and continue whisking until the mayonnaise thickens. Store for up to 2 weeks, covered, in the refrigerator.

# AIOLI

*Makes about ½ cup*

## ⊰ INGREDIENTS ⊱

- ½ cup mayonnaise (see above)
- 4 garlic cloves

1. Gather your ingredients.

2. Crush the garlic into a paste with the blunt side of the knife.

3. Whisk the garlic and mayonnaise together in a small bowl. Store for up to 2 weeks, covered, in the refrigerator.

# TOMATO SAUCE

## SAUCE TOMATE

*Makes about 3 cups*

This sauce plays on the flavors of the other vegetables as much as it does on the tomatoes.
It is a Provençal recipe that can be a base for many dishes, including pasta, polenta, chicken, and fish.

### ‹ INGREDIENTS ›

- ½ onion
- 1 carrot
- 1 celery rib
- 2 garlic cloves
- 5 tomatoes
- 1 tablespoon extra-virgin olive oil
- 2 tablespoons tomato paste
- 3 sprigs fresh thyme
- 5 fresh basil leaves
- ½ cup water
- Salt and freshly ground pepper

1. Gather your ingredients.

2. Finely chop the onion, carrot, celery, and garlic.

3. Bring a medium saucepan filled with water to boil and add the tomatoes. Remove after 30 seconds and plunge into an ice water bath.

4. With a paring knife, peel the tomatoes.

5. Cut the tomatoes in half and discard the seeds.

6. Finely chop the tomatoes.

7. In a medium pot over medium heat, heat the olive oil and add the garlic, celery, carrot, and onion. Cook for 3 to 5 minutes, or until slightly softened.

8. Add the tomatoes, tomato paste, thyme, basil, and water. Cook, stirring, for 5 to 7 minutes.

9. In batches, blend the sauce to your desired consistency (chunky or smooth). Season to taste with salt and pepper. Store, covered, for up to 1 week in the refrigerator or 1 month in the freezer.

# BÉCHAMEL SAUCE

*Makes about 1½ cups*

### ⊰ INGREDIENTS ⊱

- 2 tablespoons unsalted butter
- 3 tablespoons all-purpose flour
- 1 cup cold milk
- 1 teaspoon ground nutmeg
- Salt and freshly ground pepper

1. Gather your ingredients.

2. In a sauté pan over medium-low heat, melt the butter. Add the flour and whisk until they are combined.

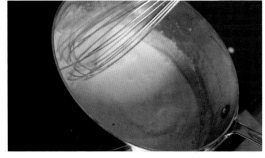

3. Whisk in the milk slowly and cook, whisking constantly, for 10 to 15 minutes, until thick. Add the nutmeg, salt, and pepper. Store, covered, in the refrigerator for 4 to 5 days.

### ⊰ KITCHEN NOTES ⊱
- Add shredded cheese before adding the salt and pepper.
- Béchamel is great on poached eggs with spinach.

# HOLLANDAISE SAUCE

*Makes about 1 cup*

### ⊰ INGREDIENTS ⊱

- 1 tablespoon water
- 4 egg yolks
- ¾ cup (1½ sticks) unsalted butter, melted and clarified
- to separate the white solids from the yellow liquid
- Juice of ½ lemon
- Salt and freshly ground pepper

1. Gather your ingredients.

2. In a stainless-steel saucepan, just barely warm and over low heat, combine the water and egg yolks. Cook, whisking constantly, for 8 minutes or until thick (you should be able to see the bottom of the pan while whisking).

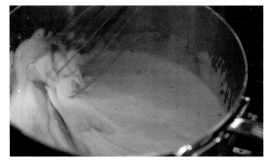

3. Add the clarified butter while continuing to whisk. Finally, whisk in the lemon juice, salt, and pepper.

# PESTO

*Makes 1 cup*

### ◄ INGREDIENTS ►

- 1 large bunch basil
- 2½ ounces Parmesan cheese, grated
- 3 tablespoons pine nuts
- ⅓ cup extra-virgin olive oil
- 2 garlic cloves

1. Gather your ingredients.

2. Chop the stems off the basil. Combine all the ingredients in a blender and puree.

3. To thin the pesto, add more olive oil.

### ◄ KITCHEN NOTES ►

- Store as is for 3 to 4 days. To keep longer, cover with a layer of olive oil to seal off from air.

# PISTOU

*Makes 1 cup*

### ◄ INGREDIENTS ►

- 1 large bunch fresh basil
- ¾ cup extra-virgin olive oil
- 4 garlic cloves
- Salt and freshly ground pepper

1. Gather your ingredients.

2. Stem the basil, combine all the ingredients in a blender, and puree.

3. For a thinner consistency, add more olive oil. Store as is in the refrigerator for 3 to 4 days, or cover with a layer of olive oil and store for up to 2 weeks.

# JUS DE CRUSTACÉS

*Makes ¾ cup*

This Mediterranean stock is widely used in French cuisine. We use it in some of our monthly specials. It is essentially a shrimp stock, made with shrimp heads. Don't be alarmed, though—the applications are endless for this rich, fruity base.

## ◄ INGREDIENTS ►

- 1 tablespoon unsalted butter or extra-virgin olive oil
- ½ onion, sliced
- 3 garlic cloves
- 9 ounces shrimp heads, coarsely chopped
- 2 tablespoons tomato paste
- ¼ cup pastis
- 4 fennel ribs
- 1 tomato, cut into wedges
- 2 cups water
- 3 or 4 sprigs fresh basil
- Salt and freshly ground pepper

1. Gather your ingredients.

2. Melt the butter in a pot over high heat and add the onion, garlic, and shrimp heads. Cook for 1 to 2 minutes, stirring.

3. Add the tomato paste and continue to cook for 3 to 4 minutes, stirring. Add the pastis, stir, and flambé: Tilt the saucepan so the pastis nears the edge and let the flame catch it (a match will do if you're not cooking with gas).

4. Immediately after the flame dies, add the fennel and tomato. Cook for 1 minute to reduce the pastis. Add the water and cook, uncovered, for 20 minutes. Add the basil and stir.

5. Over a large bowl, strain the mix, using a wooden spatula to press out all the liquid.

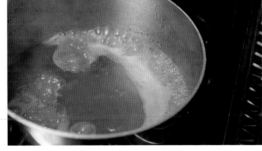

6. Transfer the liquid to a saucepan. Bring to a boil over high heat and continue boiling to reduce the liquid by half, about 5 to 7 minutes. Add salt and pepper to taste. Store, covered, in the refrigerator for 5 days.

## ◄ KITCHEN NOTES ►

- For a vinaigrette, reduce again by half to get about 2 tablespoons stock. Add 1 tablespoon vinegar and 1 tablespoon olive oil.
- This *jus* can be made using any crustacean head, such as lobster or crab, by following the same process.
- For all sauces—when refrigerating, use two layers of plastic wrap: one that lays on top of the liquid, sealing it, and the other that drapes over the entire container.

# LAMB JUS

## JUS D'AGNEAU

*❯❮*

*Makes 4 cups*

This can be used as a sauce or as a base for cooking lamb or veggies.

❮ INGREDIENTS ❯

- 3 pounds lamb on the bone
- ½ cup (1 stick) unsalted butter
- 1 garlic bulb
- 2 shallots
- 3 bay leaves
- 2 sprigs fresh thyme
- 5 cups chicken broth

1. Gather your ingredients. Cut the entire garlic bulb in half. Peel and thinly slice the shallots.

2. In a large pot over medium-high heat, brown the lamb. Remove the lamb and set aside.

3. In the same pot, melt the butter and add the garlic, shallots, bay leaves, and thyme. Sauté for 2 to 3 minutes.

4. Return the lamb to the pot and cover with water.

5. Bring to a boil, reduce the heat to medium, and cook for about 1 hour, until the water has almost completely evaporated.

6. Repeat step 5 two more times, adding fresh water and reducing it. Using a brush, scrape the sides of the pot to incorporate the *suc*, bits on the side after each reduction.

7. Repeat step 5 a third and final time using the chicken broth instead of water.

8. Strain the liquid into a large bowl.

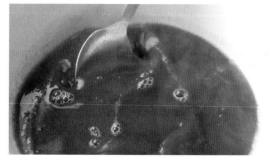

9. Transfer the liquid to a saucepan and heat over medium heat to liquefy. Cool, transfer to an ice cube tray, and freeze. Or, of course, use right away!

❮ KITCHEN NOTES ❯

· The more you reduce, the more concentrated the flavor of the stock will be.

La Boulange Café Cooking at Home

# MUSHROOM SAUCE

## SAUCE AUX CHAMPIGNONS

*Makes 2 cups*

### ⊰ INGREDIENTS ⊱

- 4 big portobello mushrooms
- 2 shallots
- 2 garlic cloves
- 2 tablespoons extra-virgin olive oil
- ½ cup white wine
- 1 cup heavy cream
- Salt and freshly ground pepper

1. Gather your ingredients.

2. Prepare the mushrooms by removing the stems and peeling the skin off the rounded side of each cap.

3. Slice the mushroom caps. Peel and chop the shallots and garlic.

4. In a large sauté pan over medium heat, heat the olive oil and add the shallots and garlic. Sweat for about 2 minutes without browning. Add the mushrooms and cook for 2 minutes more.

5. Add the white wine and reduce for about 2 minutes. Add the cream and cook for another 5 to 7 minutes. Add salt and pepper to taste.

6. Transfer to a blender and puree until smooth. Store, covered, in the refrigerator for up to 1½ to 2 weeks.

### ⊰ KITCHEN NOTES ⊱

- This is a great condiment for sandwiches.
- You can add pieces of sautéed mushroom for texture.
- The sauce is wonderful inside crêpes or a vegetable tart.

# MERCI BEAUCOUP

*Merci beaucoup,*
all of our wonderful customers,
and our incredibly talented staff:
the bakers
the pastry chefs
the chefs
the cooks
the dishwashers
the packers
the drivers
the retail staff
the baristas
the general managers
the district managers
the operations team
the training team
the catering department
the administration
the controller
the CFO
the HR Department
the Sales and Marketing Department
the designers and artists
the Quality Control
the Repair and Maintenance
the construction team—
all 900 of you, as of today.
A thank you to our dedicated suppliers:
the farmers
the millers
the dairies
the meat and poultry producers
the fair trade chocolate makers
the coffee growers and roasters
the distributors, local and national (we like them all).

In addition to each and every one of the people I just mentioned who give life to La Boulange Café and Bakery every day, the small and nimble group below brought all the pieces together and made this book happen, right above the mother bakery on Pine Street in San Francisco:

David Vergne, our photographer, Alain Bourgade, our chef de cuisine, Stephane Stocki, our pastry chef, and Leah Donnelly, our book producer. Thank you also to J. C. Hurtado, Leo Valenzuela, Rita Treanor, Mehdi Boudiab, Rona Vergne, and Arthur Aravena. Our recipe testers—thank you for testing and for your diligent and thoughtful feedback:

Marinda Scott and Amy Hinson
Jeppe and Diana Paustian
Rona Vergne
Caitlin Welch
Nancy and Philip Donnelly
Anna Donnelly and Jason Rothman
Amanda Kropelnicki
Tessa Niles
Camille Byrne
Mario Pimenta
Paul Primozich
Tom Bensel
Peter Judd and Kelly Waters
Marie Knapp
Dawn Yanagihara
Levi Hunt
Katie Solinger

*Merci Beaucoup*

# INDEX